The Pig War
Conflict and Resolution
in the Pacific Northwest

Project Coordinator/Editor: Mike Vouri
Curriculum Development: Janet Oakley
Evaluator: Richard Vanderway

For Information:

(360) 378-2902

(360) 378-2240

FAX: (360) 378-2615

EMAIL: sajh_interpretation@NPS.gov

Acknowledgments

This traveling trunk and curriculum program was made possible through a grant from the **National Park Foundation**. Additional contributions of time and materials were made by Ms. Sharon Ingram, Mr. Matt Boswell, Mr. Richard Vanderway and Chief Ranger Bill Gleason.

Welcome

What is this "Pig War" all about? Why do we need a park about it? These are questions most often asked by park visitors from outside the Northwest Washington region. When they learn that Great Britain and the United States almost plunged into war over a dead pig, the initial reaction is amusement. After all, 19th century journalists did label the dispute with tongue in cheek. The challenge for our interpreters is to demonstrate that here was one of those rare occasions when two nations chose to avoid war at all costs by opting for diplomacy and eventually binding arbitration; where restraint was demonstrated from the halls of power to the men in the ranks; and a lasting peace was assured along more than 3,000 miles of international border.

Thanks to a grant from the National Park Foundation, San Juan Island National Historical Park is now able to deliver this message to the doorsteps of schools throughout Washington State. *The Pig War Conflict and Resolution in the Pacific Northwest* curriculum and traveling trunk program is designed especially for 4th/5th grade students whose curriculum includes Washington State history, but can be utilized at all grade levels. The package also includes an introduction to mediation techniques designed to maintain peace in the hallways and at home. The curriculum and traveling trunk offer a unique opportunity to underscore both topics through exercises, exhibits and handouts that are entertaining as well as thought-provoking.

We hope the curriculum and trunk fulfill your needs and that you find it as exciting and challenging to present as it was for us to assemble. You can help us improve the guide by filling out the evaluation in the back of this guide.

Thanks for allowing San Juan Island National Historical Park to become part of your educational experience.

Sincerely,

Peter Dederich
Superintendent

San Juan Island
National Historical Park

ABOUT THIS RESOURCE GUIDE

In the summer of 1859, the legend of the Oregon Trail was already sixteen years old. Darwin's On the Origin of Species was newly published and the rumbles of the Civil War were being heard in the distance. Here in the Northwest, little communities were developing throughout the newly created Washington Territory. The survey of the U.S.-Canadian border by Great Britain and the United States had entered its third year and threats of raids by northern Indian groups had lessened. A gold strike in British Columbia saw a population boom and bust at Whatcom (present-day Bellingham, Washington). Imagine the unease when word arrived in that tiny settlement that the British were threatening to arrest an American citizen living in the San Juan Islands over the shooting of a Hudson's Bay Company pig. In a short period of time, tensions quickly escalated to the point that a small detachment of American soldiers stood face to face against the greatest naval force in the world, the British Royal Navy. Unknown to their respective leaders thousands of miles away, a war was brewing. Only when cooler heads prevailed did the conflict come to a peaceful resolution.

Nearly a century and a half later, the conflict is remembered as the "Pig War," although there never was a war. There have been other misconceptions as well. The purpose of this trunk program and curriculum is to provide teachers and students with hands-on activities and materials to better understand this important historic event. Beyond the war's quaint title, there is a deeper lesson: that people can and should take every opportunity to stop and listen to one another and to employ peaceful means to resolve conflicts. In this vein, the Pig War traveling trunk is designed to achieve the following

GOALS:

- ◆ Increase students' knowledge of the events and issues from 1853-74 surrounding the boundary dispute, the Pig War, and the joint occupation of San Juan Island.

- ◆ Increase students' knowledge of the geography of the area and its relationship to the argument over the international water boundary.

- ◆ Develop an appreciation for the life of the common soldier who was a part of the arbitration/occupation of San Juan Island.

- ◆ Develop an appreciation for the historic attempts to defuse the volatile situation on San Juan Island and current methods for conflict resolution on the playground, in the classroom and at home.

ABOUT THE TRAVELING TRUNK PROGRAM

The program is a curriculum-trunk including:

* A full curriculum unit with laminated support materials.

* Artifacts for making a mini-museum.

* Interpretive materials.

. The program is divided into six units:

1. Setting the Stage

This unit includes information on the geography of the area, the Oregon Treaty of 1846, issues leading up to the crisis, the main British and American claims, the establishment of the Hudson's Bay Company's Bellevue Farm and its impact on American settlers in the Pacific Northwest and on San Juan Island. Students learn geography by identifying locations on maps and correctly ordering mix-and-match charts.

2. A Pig Takes the Stage

This unit features the personal relationships between Bellevue Farm manager Charles Griffin and American settler Lyman Cutlar, the principle antagonists. Students explore alternatives and learn to make choices through thought-provoking exercises, including role-playing. Also included is information about the famous Berkshire boar, fragments from the Bellevue Farm diary and biographies of Griffin and Cutlar.

3. The Cast Increases

Mediation and conflict management techniques are taught through role-playing to illustrate how the arrival of British and American civil and military officials complicated matters. Students consult the players' sheet and determine how each individual would have reacted to the Pig War crisis and other situations. The unit also includes the biographies of British Columbia Governor James Douglas, U.S. Army Brigadier General William S. Harney, U.S. Army Captain George Pickett, Royal Navy Captain Geoffrey Phipps Hornby, as well as other important players.

4. Finding a Solution

Military and governmental proposals for resolving the crisis are reviewed, including the British and American views. Students have an opportunity to refine their role-playing techniques by resolving their own issues. One exercise requires exchanging messages between groups.

5. Keeping the Peace 1859-1872

The experiences of the common soldiers and officers at American Camp and their counterparts in the Royal Marines are explored, including social contacts between the two groups. Students can read correspondence from a boy who lived at American Camp in the 1860s and compare their lives with his; they also can use games, such as "Red Light, Green Light," to learn more about how simple rules can keep a situation from spinning out of control.

6. Settling the Claim

Students are encouraged to write about a problem they might be having in the classroom or at home and think about different solutions, including the introduction of a third party mediator such as Kaiser Wilhelm, who decided the fate of the San Juan Islands. The boundary commissioner's role in all of this is also examined, as well as the fate of the camps and the final good-byes between the U.S. Army and the Royal Marines.

For those who do not wish to use the trunk, a curriculum-only packet is available upon request.

ESSENTIAL LEARNINGS:

The Pig War program meets the Washington State Essential Learnings requirements for social studies.

Subjects	Topics
History	Biographies of key historical figures
	Hudson's Bay Company
	Pig War events
	American and English camps
	Timeline

Oregon Treaty of 1846
Boundary survey of 1858-1862

Geography   Maps of Pacific Northwest, San Juan Islands
Location of military camps, principal island roads
Settler claims and Hudson's Bay property
Features of San Juan Island
Weather, topography, natural resources

Civics   Arbitration
Conflict resolution
Martial law vs. civil government
Relationships between military camps and settlers
Citizenship under joint occupancy
Property rights under joint occupancy
San Juan Village

Economics   Clothing and food rations
Laundress/soldiers
Bellevue Farm livestock/acreage

The Pig War program also addresses some of the essential learnings for language arts:

Using different texts   Letters from the H.A. Allen collection
Reading for meaning   The journal of Private William A. Peck, U.S. Army
Predicting outcomes   The journal of A.W. Joy, Royal Marines

IMPLEMENTING THE PIG WAR CURRICULUM

The Pig War curriculum is a multi-faceted program designed for use with the traveling trunk or as a stand-alone social studies unit. In each case, with or without the trunk, the curriculum can be implemented in several ways depending on the time allowed in the classroom. The curriculum can be implemented in the following strands or areas of emphasis:

1.   The Complete Curriculum

Reviewed on the previous pages, the curriculum can be presented over a 10-day period, 30-40 minutes per lesson time. Begin with **Setting the Stage** on page 6, introducing the maps and background to the boundary dispute. Follow through with the issues and main players in the events behind the Pig War and its settlement. A shorter version would include Units 1-6, using text for lecture and the biographies of main characters for study. It can be done in a fourth grade classroom in about five days.

2.   Conflict and Resolution

How do people and nations resolve conflict? This focus begins with a complete study of **Setting the Stage** (Unit 1, page 6) and concentrates on the **Settling Arguments** lessons of each unit. Use the chart on page 35 to provide background information on main players in the initial crisis. Use pictures, maps and biographies for interest and visual support. Five to six days.

3.   Journals and Letters: The Language of the Times

Throughout the curriculum, there are journal entries and letters from 1859 -1872. Begin with **Setting the Stage** (Unit 1, p. 6). Talk about 19th century habit of keeping journals and writing letters. Use text and activities in **Journals as History and Letters as History** (pp. 85-94). Use knowledge to locate other letters and journal entries in the curriculum. The Bellevue diaries are especially interesting (pp. 26-30). Write your own journals. Four to five days.

4.   Soldiering in the Pacific Northwest (1859-1872)

San Juan Island was occupied by British and American troops during the Civil War. Explore army life at American Camp using **Setting the Stage** (Unit 1, p. 6) for background. Read the **Project of a Temporary Settlement** on p. 59 and Units 5 (pp. 61-94). The joint military occupation is a fascinating part of Northwest history that is appealing to students. Classrooms can visit the actual American and English camps on San Juan Island through San Juan Island Historical National Park. Park personnel can provide a tour and activities for the students upon request. Three to four days.

Unit One

Setting
the Stage

SETTING THE STAGE

Have you ever had an argument with a friend over something you both wanted and before you knew it, the little argument became a big argument?

The Pig War of 1859 wasn't really a war over a pig, but a loud disagreement that almost came to fighting over a much more important issue between Great Britain and the United States. What they both wanted was the group of 175 named islands known as the San Juan Islands. These islands lay between Vancouver Island on the west and what is the mainland of Washington State today on the east. These islands were once a part of the **Oregon Country**.

Oregon Country is the name of the area of the continent of North America that once included the present-day states of Oregon, Washington, Idaho and the Canadian province of British Columbia, plus portions of the states of Wyoming and Montana. Since the 1790s, Great Britain and the United States had been interested in the area. The British explored it for fur trading and timber. Under Royal Navy Captain George Vancouver in 1792, Puget Sound was explored and many of its features and islands named. American President Thomas Jefferson sent Meriwether Lewis and William Clark in 1804 to learn about its resources and the people who lived along the Columbia River. It took two years for the Lewis and Clark party to travel from St. Louis to the Oregon coast and return. A few years later, fur-trading was attempted by some Americans on the coast of Oregon near the river, but hard times made their venture fail. Still, the United States and Great Britain each wanted to claim Oregon. Both countries were growing. The United States was being settled in Illinois and Indiana, while the British were expanding above the Great Lakes in Canada. Sometimes they argued about the boundaries between them. In fact, they had even fought battles over what was American or British and what was not. These battles were called the War of 1812.

In 1814, Great Britain signed a landmark peace treaty with the United States. It was called the Treaty of Ghent. It ended the War of 1812 and said that the existing U.S.-Canada boundary that went from northern Maine to the Great Lakes would always be the boundary between the two countries. There would be no more fighting.

In 1818, the United States and Britain agreed to a **"Convention of Commerce,"** which set the boundary between the United States and British North America from the "northwest angle of Lake of the Woods, Minnesota, to the **49° parallel** of north latitude, thence west to Stony Mountains" (the Rocky Mountains). It further stated that both the United States and Great Britain would occupy the Oregon Country.

However, in 1818, the Oregon Country was too far away for Americans to settle and nearly so for the British, except for the **Hudson's Bay Company**, a British-owned fur trading giant that would dominate the area for the next 20 years.

In 1846, the British and the United States signed another important treaty. It was called the **Treaty of Oregon**. By now, many changes had happened in the Oregon Country. Since 1824, the

Hudson's Bay Company had engaged in a brisk trade for otter pelts with the native peoples of the Northwest: from the Chinook on the Columbia River to the Haida, Tlingit and other Northwest Coast groups as far north as Russian America. From furs, the company early expanded into timber, farming and fishing, industries that would dominate in the Pacific Northwest into the late 20th century. The Hudson's Bay Company built forts in several areas of the Northwest and even brought a paddle wheel steamboat over from London. Their only purpose was to trade, not to settle. For many years **Fort Vancouver** on the Columbia River was the main center of British power. Then in 1837, American missionaries came to the Northwest and settled in Walla Walla, Washington. They encouraged other Americans to come. In 1843, the first great wagon train left for the Oregon Trail and soon many more Americans would come to the Oregon Country. That same year, the Hudson's Bay Company founded **Fort Victoria** on Vancouver Island.

The Treaty of Oregon was important because it said that the 49th parallel would once again divide the United States from the territories and colonies of Great Britain. All of the old Oregon Country below the 49th parallel would become part of the United States. All of Vancouver Island went to the British. All Hudson's Bay Company property south of the 49th parallel would belong to the United States, and British citizens living in the new Oregon Territory would be protected. It was a good treaty except for one problem. It told only where the **land boundary** would be. It did not say exactly where the **water boundary** should be between Vancouver Island and the mainland of Washington Territory. All it said was that the boundary would be "the middle of the channel which separates the continent from the Vancouver's Island." The treaty signers were vaguely aware that there were two channels— Haro Strait to the west, near Vancouver Island and Rosario Strait to the east, near the mainland. If the international boundary went through Haro Strait, the Americans would get the San Juan Islands. If it went through Rosario Strait, the British would own them. However, in the interest of keeping the peace, they were in a hurry to sign the treaty. They figured the boundary would somehow take care of itself. But it was not to be. Thirteen years later, a British pig would wander into an American potato patch on San Juan Island, setting off the event called the Pig War.

The S.S. *Beaver*

SETTING THE STAGE QUIZ

NAME_____

Several important treaties, people and events helped shape the history of the Pacific Northwest before the Pig War. In the chart below, fill in the boxes with information you read in "Setting the Stage." In the last set of boxes below, explain which subjects you want to know more about and why.

What/ who is it?	Date	What do you know?
Oregon Country	1818-1846	
	1814	Treaty between the United States and Great Britain; ended War of 1812.
	1846	
Hudson's Bay Company		
		Explored the Northwest for America. Went down the Columbia River to the Oregon coast.
49th Parallel	First used 1818	

THE PACIFIC NORTHWEST IN 1859

The Pacific Northwest in 1859 had gone through some more changes—again. From the time the Treaty of Oregon was signed in 1846 to the summer of 1859, the old Oregon Country had been split up several times. First, the Oregon Territory was created. It included all the land below the 49th parallel to the 41st parallel (near California). In 1853, the Oregon Territory was split into two territories above and below the Columbia River. Oregon was below the river. Washington Territory was formed above the Columbia River and included Idaho and parts of Montana. Vancouver Island on the British side changed too. It had been under a "charter" with the Hudson's Bay Company, but in 1849 it became a Crown Colony, which allowed settlers to come. Ten years later the area north of the 49th parallel became a Crown Colony too — British Columbia. Oregon became a state in 1859.

1. Look at the map of the Pacific Northwest 1859. Find and label the following:

Columbia River	49th parallel
Fort Victoria	Seattle
Olympia	Fort Vancouver
Fort Bellingham	

2. Color the British colonies turquoise.

3   Color Washington Territory light red.

4   Color Oregon a light purple.

5. Color the San Juan Islands orange.

6. Getting around the Pacific Northwest was different in 1859. There were no trains, cars or even good wagon roads. People walked on trails made by Indians or they went by water. There were steamboats, but they could cost money, so people often went great distances by canoe or by rowing. Look at the map again. Using the scale of miles, find out how far is was from:

Fort Vancouver to Victoria _____ miles

Fort Bellingham to Seattle _____ miles

Victoria to the San Juan Islands _____ miles

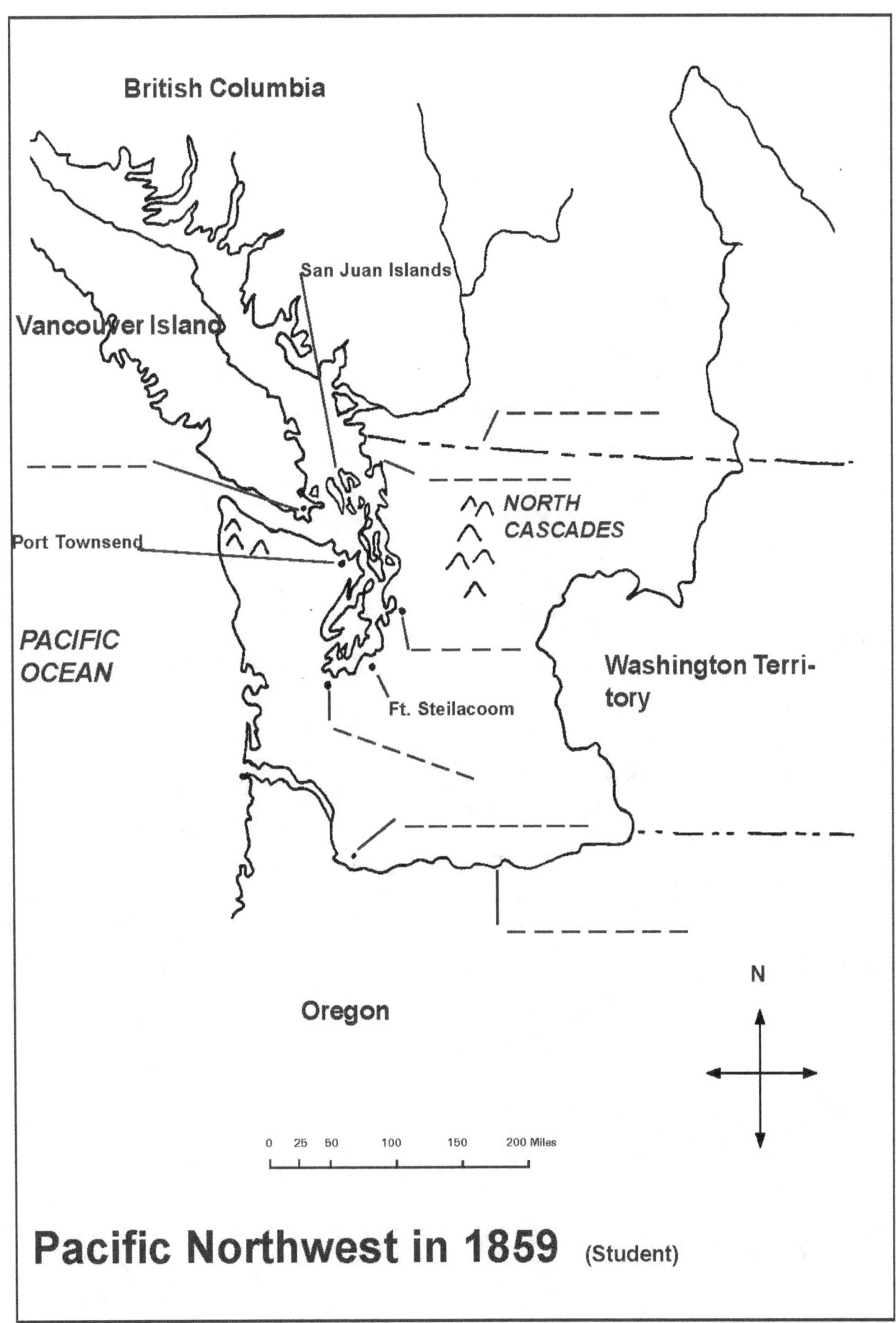

British Columbia

San Juan Islands

Vancouver Island

NORTH
CASCADES

Port Townsend

PACIFIC
OCEAN

Ft. Steilacoom

Washington Terri-
tory

Oregon

N

0   25   50   100   150   200 Miles

Pacific Northwest in 1859 (Student)

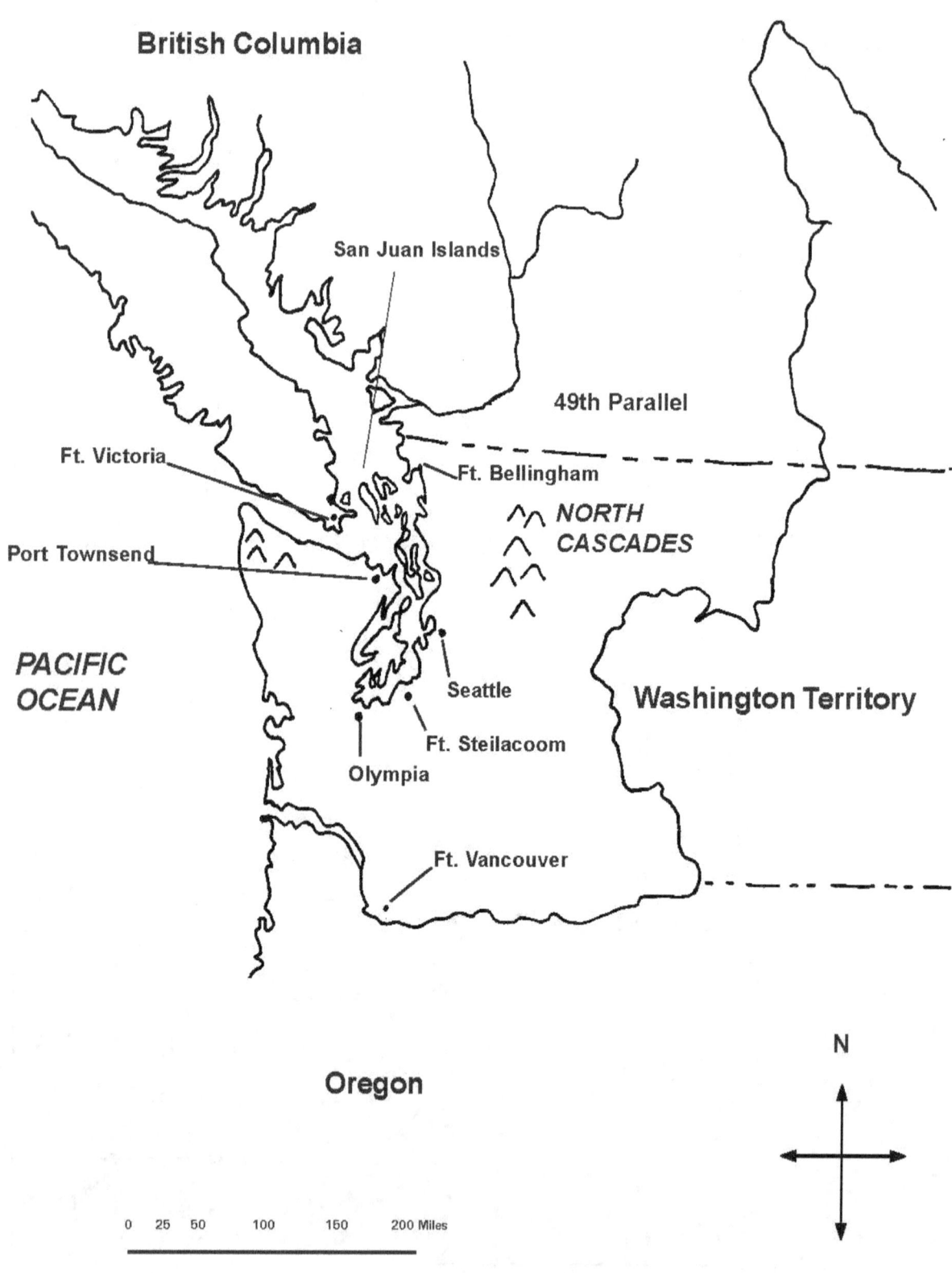

British Columbia

San Juan Islands

49th Parallel

Ft. Victoria

Ft. Bellingham

Port Townsend

NORTH CASCADES

PACIFIC OCEAN

Seattle

Washington Territory

Ft. Steilacoom

Olympia

Ft. Vancouver

Oregon

N

0 25 50   100   150   200 Miles

Pacific Northwest in 1859 (Teacher)

THE ISLANDS IN QUESTION

The San Juan Islands are made up of 175 named islands and islets located between Vancouver Island on the west and the mainland of northwestern Washington State on the east. They are about 25 miles across. To their north is the Canadian Strait of Georgia. To their south is the American Strait of Juan de Fuca. In the 1850s, they were wild places, with deep forests and wind-swept prairies. The islands proved excellent fishing grounds and had been the winter home of the Lummi People and other Indians for many years. However, they were not a friendly place for white settlers or Indians in the 1850s because of the great "northern tribes," warring Haida and Tlingit Indians who came from present-day Southeast Alaska and British Columbia to raid. People did not stay long.

When the Oregon Treaty of 1846 was being written to establish the international boundary, the British government in London didn't know very much about the geography of the area. Their maps were 50 years old. However, the Hudson's Bay Company did know a good deal about the islands and they knew about Rosario and Haro straits. Since 1827, they had come through these straits on their way to the Fraser River in today's British Columbia where they had an important fort. The S.S. *Beaver*, their side-wheel paddle steamboat, usually went through Haro Strait, which was the best passage for boats. But when the treaty was written, the "channel" was not named. The Hudson's Bay Company, which knew better, believed that the boundary must be made along the Rosario Strait, even though their steamboat didn't go that way very often. They knew it was the only way for Britain to get all the islands.

1.   Look at the maps of the islands. Find the following:

Strait of Georgia   Vancouver Island
Strait of Juan de Fuca   Haro Strait
San Juan Island   San Juan Channel
Rosario Strait

2.   Color the boundary line the British wanted red.

3.   Color the boundary line the Americans wanted blue.

4.   In the 1850s, the British and Americans traveled by steam or sail on the water. A steamboat could negotiate the San Juan Channel with no problems, provided it did not draw too much water. It was quite another story for sailing ships, howver, which is why it was not given serious consideration as the boundary channel. Why would this channel present problems for sailing ships?

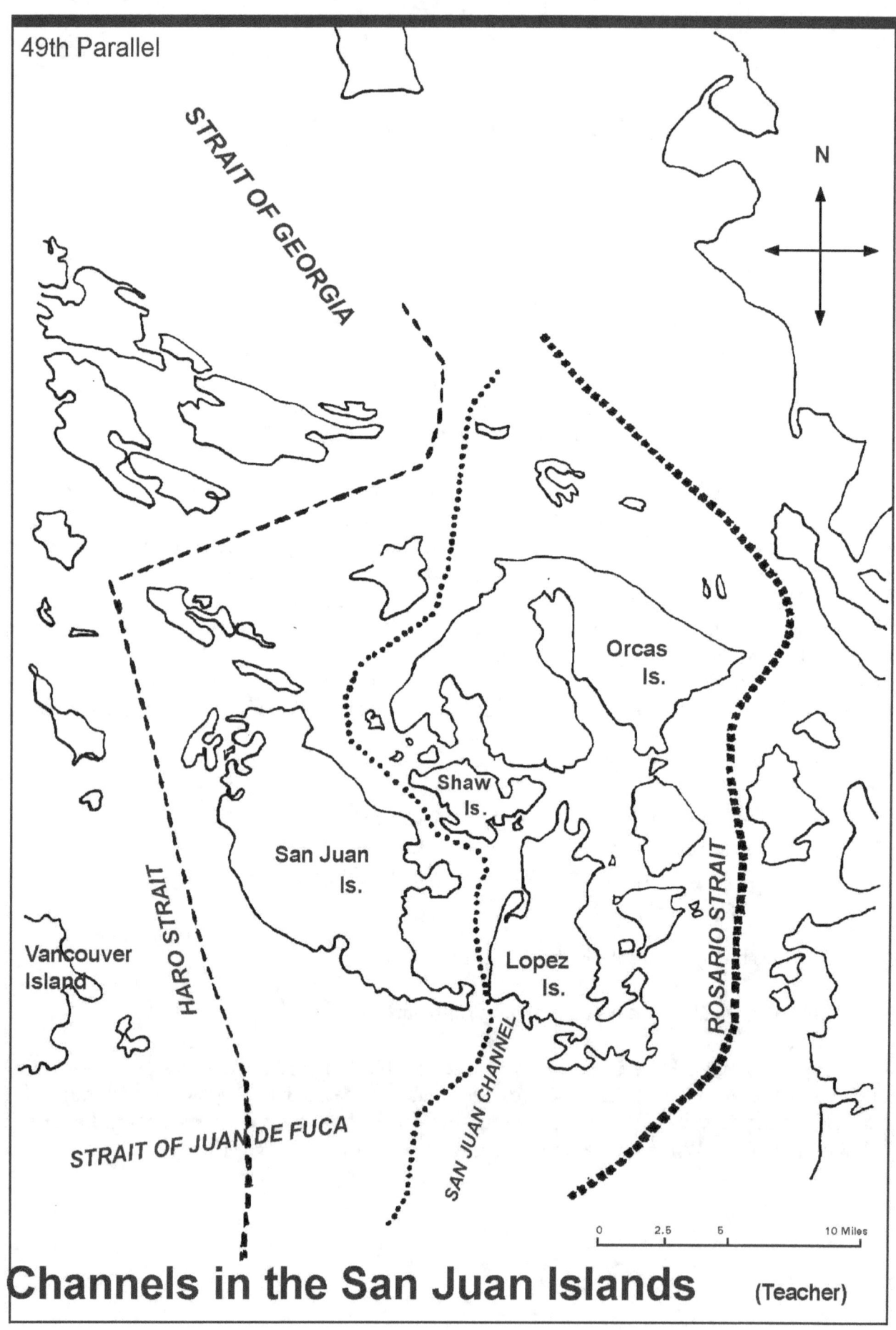

49th Parallel

STRAIT OF GEORGIA

N

STRAIT OF JUAN DE FUCA

HARO STRAIT

Vancouver
Island

San Juan
Is.

Shaw
Is.

Orcas
Is.

Lopez
Is.

SAN JUAN CHANNEL

ROSARIO STRAIT

0   2.5   5   10 Miles

Channels in the San Juan Islands (Teacher)

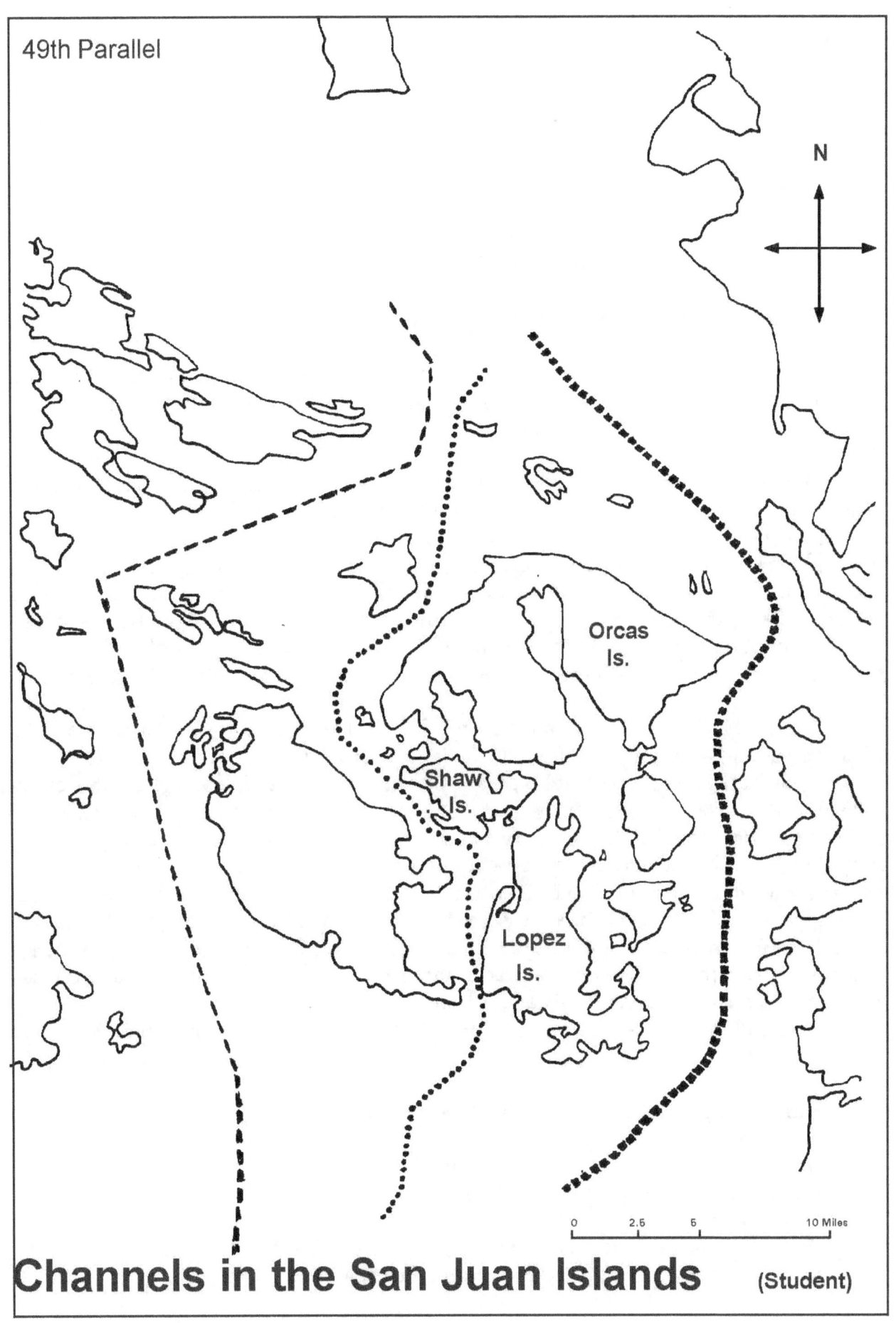

49th Parallel

N

Orcas
Is.

Shaw
Is.

Lopez
Is.

0   2.5   5   10 Miles

Channels in the San Juan Islands (Student)

SAN JUAN ISLAND

San Juan Island is the second largest island in the San Juan Islands. It was the closest to Fort Victoria on Vancouver Island (15 miles away). Like many of the islands, it was largely covered with great forests with a few small ponds and meadows, but on its southern end it was hilly and more open. San Juan Island was not a very good place for farming, but it was good for grazing cattle and sheep.

The **Hudson's Bay Company** had become interested in the San Juan Islands before the signing of the Oregon treaty, but after 1846, they made serious attempts to claim them. In 1848, a British map was made showing the boundary passing through Rosario Strait. When Vancouver Island was given to the company a year later, its new leader, **James Douglas,** looked for ways to bring the islands into the company's empire.

Douglas began his efforts in 1850 and 1851 when he had a fishing station set up on San Juan Island during the summer. Here salmon could be salted and put into barrels. Several Indians worked for the company, which paid them in blankets. Horses were left behind during the winter. In 1853, a more serious attempt was made. Douglas did not want Americans coming and "squatting" (settling illegally) in the islands. On the night of December 13, **Charles J. Griffin** and a band of Hawaiian shepherds who worked for the company, along with 1300 sheep, landed on the southern end of the island. Here they would set up a sheep ranch called **Bellevue Farm** on the Strait of Juan de Fuca side of the Cattle Point peninsula. Across the peninsula, on the more sheltered **Griffin Bay** shore, Griffin built a ship **wharf.**

The Americans, of course, were not happy. They had been claiming the islands since 1848. When Washington Territory was created in 1853, San Juan Island was a part of it. When they heard about the sheep at Bellevue Farm, they sent a tax collector over from the little village of Whatcom on Bellingham Bay to collect taxes on the sheep. The British refused to pay and the Americans confiscated 35 breeding rams, which resulted in a protest to the President of the United States. Bellevue Farm endured, however, and continued to send wool to various forts around the northwest. As for the Americans, not many wanted to live on San Juan Island. They were afraid of the fierce northern Indians. Those that did come to the island chose to live near Bellevue Farm. For one, those lands were more suitable for farming because of the open prairies; for another, the Indians would not dare attack a Hudson's Bay Company facility backed by the might of the Royal Navy. Then in 1859 an American miner named **Lyman Cutlar** came to the island, built a hut and planted a potato patch a mile and a half northwest of Bellevue Farm — right in the middle of Charles Griffin's main sheep run. Griffin was furious and soon so was Cutlar.

1.   Find and mark the following on the San Juan Island map:

Griffin Bay   Bellevue Farm
Hudson's Bay Wharf   Cutlar farm

2.   Find Victoria on the Pacific Northwest Map. Using the scale of miles, how many miles from Victoria to Bellevue Farm? To Fort Bellingham?

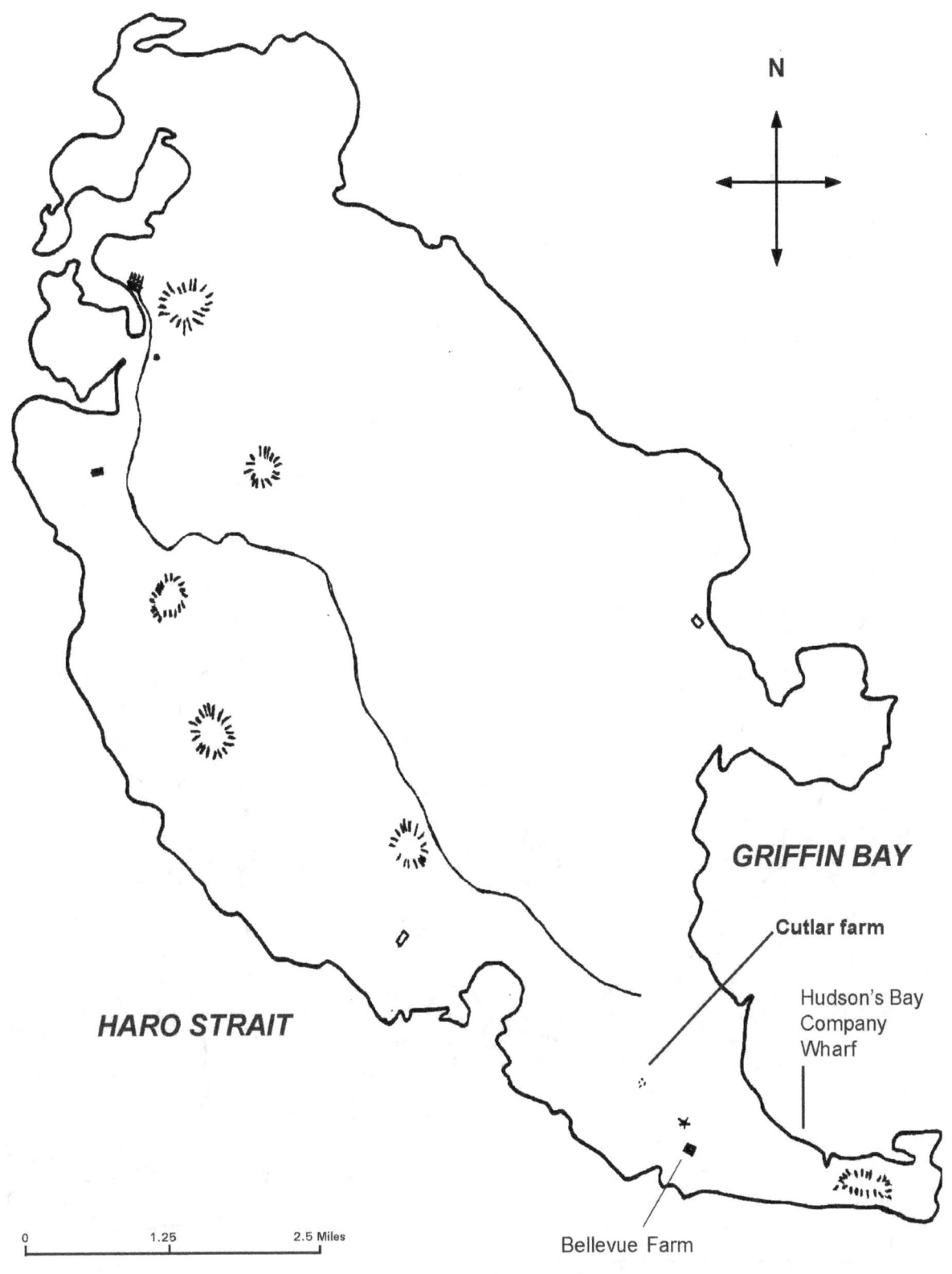

N

GRIFFIN BAY

Cutlar farm

Hudson's Bay
Company
Wharf

HARO STRAIT

0   1.25   2.5 Miles

Bellevue Farm

San Juan Island in June 1859 (Teacher)

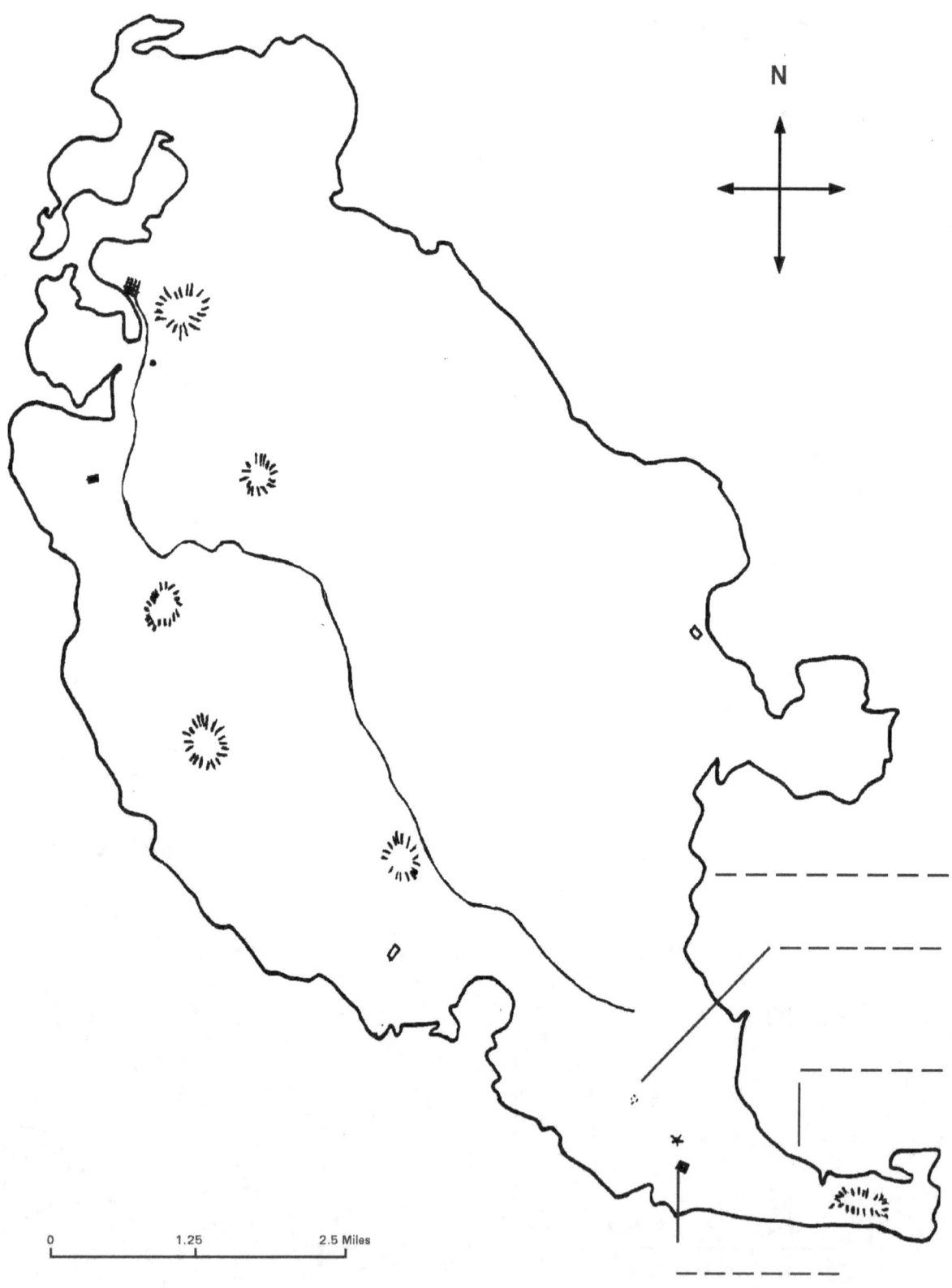

San Juan Island in June 1859 (Student)

SETTLING ARGUMENTS: COUNTRIES

When countries have an argument, one way of settling it is to sign a treaty. To do this, each side chooses a person or a group to represent them. These representatives then sit down and **negotiate** or discuss the things that they agree on and the things they don't agree on. They try to find "common ground." When they are finally in agreement, they sign and take the treaty back to their countries where the treaty is **ratified** or approved by the part of their government that makes laws. In our country, Congress ratifies treaties. Once a treaty is ratified, our country will obey what is in the treaty.

The Oregon Treaty was signed in 1846. Since a boundary is often an imaginary line, it takes scientists using special instruments to determine where it is. This is called a **survey**. However, it took years before an international boundary commission was set up to survey along the 49th parallel. In the meantime, hundreds of American settlers had come into those parts of the United States that were close to the Canadian border. In the San Juan Islands, Americans coming back from the gold fields in British Columbia were stopping off and finding places where they would like to live, but the Hudson's Bay Company was claiming the area for Great Britain. Both countries were heading for big trouble.

After the signing of the treaty, the countries did two things wrong.

◆ They didn't say **exactly** where the water boundary was going to be.

◆ They waited years before starting the survey.

A. What could the United States and Great Britain have done differently? Look at the ideas below. How would they have made a difference? On a separate piece of paper write what you think.

◆ Sign a treaty that told exactly where the water boundary was in the San Juan Islands.

◆ Start the survey of the water boundary before anyone moved in.

B. Mrs. G's 4th grade and Mr. R's 5th grade share the same playground at recess. The 5th graders think that they should have the playground equipment all to themselves since they are older. Pretend the children are countries. How might they solve this problem before fighting breaks out?

Unit Two

A Pig
Takes The
Stage

A PIG TAKES THE STAGE
SUMMER 1859

Bellevue Farm was six years old in 1859 when an American named **Lyman Cutlar** built a shack about a mile and a half north of the main buildings where Griffin lived. He put it in the middle of one of the farm's best sheep runs, then rowed over to the Olympic Peninsula and bought some potatoes to plant. He hoped to have "taters" to eat along with what venison he could get by hunting. But when the potatoes started coming up in June, a large, black pig wandered over from the Hudson's Bay Company farm to root in the patch. Sometimes Cutlar would shoo the pig away with a switch, but it would come back. Eventually, he made a fence around the patch, but it had only three sides and the pig still got into the garden. Three times he went to see Griffin and complain. Griffin came and looked at the fence and said that it wasn't very strong. Since Griffin felt that the American shouldn't have a farm on land the British claimed, he felt that the pig was Cutlar's problem. The pig had a right to roam, he said.

On June 15, Cutlar had had enough. Awakened by noises outside, he found the boar once again feasting in his garden. Cutlar took his shotgun outside and shot the pig. A little later, feeling sorry for his actions, he went down and spoke to Griffin, offering to pay for the boar— $10 — or give him one of his own pigs. Ten dollars was a lot of money in those days, but Griffin was angry. It wasn't enough. The pig was a "valuable boar" used for breeding. Griffin asked for a hundred dollars. Cutlar said that there was a "better chance for lightning to strike you than for you to get a hundred dollars for that hog." He did offer to have a third party help settle their differences, but Griffin didn't want that. Cutlar left and went back to his farm.

The following morning, several men on horseback showed up at Cutlar's shack. They were from the Hudson's Bay Company headquarters on Vancouver Island. One of them was **A.G. Dallas**. He was in charge of Fort Victoria and the son-in-law of Governor Douglas of the Crown Colony of Vancouver Island. They had come over on the Hudson's Bay Company steamer *Beaver* to visit. Dallas asked Cutlar if he was the one who shot the pig. Cutlar said yes. He told Cutlar that if he didn't pay the $100 that he would have to go to Victoria for trial. Not long after that, a story got out that the Hudson's Bay Company had threatened to arrest an American for killing a British pig . An argument between two people had now become more serious—it now involved two nations.

SETTLING ARGUMENTS: TWO PEOPLE

Griffin and Cutlar were men from two different countries. They both thought they were right about how to settle the matter over the pig. Griffin wrote a letter to Governor Douglas on Vancouver Island the same day the pig was killed. He was not only worried about Cutlar threatening to kill his cattle if they wandered over to the American's claim, but also about hurting the "herdsmen" taking care of his sheep on that end of the island. Griffin also reported that the Americans were becoming a problem, as up to 16 squatters lived in the area, taking over the best parts of the prairie. Cutlar, on the other hand, believed he had a right to be there because the island was a part of Washington Territory, and he was a citizen of the United States. Griffin was the "foreigner" with the invalid claim as far as he was concerned. However, when Cutlar approached Griffin on June 15, he stressed that he did not come to talk about who owned the island. He came to pay for the pig.

What could have been done differently? Neither man was a bad person. At the time, the British were still not happy with the way they had lost the lands south of the 49th parallel, especially Governor Douglas. They had been there first. They worried that most of the people living on Vancouver Island were Americans. They were afraid that the United States would take lands in the British colony of British Columbia too. The Americans, on the other hand, did not like the Hudson's Bay Company. They thought it was too powerful. They forgot that in the early years, the company had helped in times of crisis, even rescuing Americans from dangers. The Americans thought they could do what they wanted.

A. What do you think would have been good ways to solve this problem about the pig? Write what you think on a separate piece of paper.

B. Look at the ideas below. Would they have been a good way to solve the problem? Why or why not? Again write your answers on a separate piece of paper.

◆ Griffin accepts the payment of $10.

◆ Cutlar promises not to bother the animals from Bellevue Farm. He will not expand his claim until the United States and Great Britain settle who owns the islands. He builds a better fence.

◆ A group is put together consisting of two British citizens and two American citizens. They will decide how to prevent any new trouble.

C. You borrowed your friend's bike and damaged the rim. You have $6. What will you do? What is right? Again write your answer on a separate piece of paper.

LYMAN CUTLAR
1830?- 1874

Born in Kentucky, possibly 1830.

Went to the Fraser River in British Columbia to mine gold.

Arrived on San Juan Island in April 1859 and set up a shack about a mile and a half north and to the west of Bellevue Farm. It was in the middle of one of the more important sheep runs. It included a garden in which potatoes were grown.

Described as tall, with light hair.

Became a partner in San Juan Island Lime Company located at Lime Kiln in 1860-61.

Said to have been elected constable in 1864 by American settlers on the island.

Left San Juan Island after 1869.

Living in Blanchard, Skagit County, Washington Territory in 1871.

There is no known photograph of Lyman Cutlar

CHARLES GRIFFIN
Manager of Bellevue Farm (1853-1862)

CHARLES GRIFFIN
Manager of Bellevue Farm (1853-1862)

Very little is known of Charles Griffin before he came to San Juan Island.

He was about 30 years old in 1853. His previous job was at Fort Simpson further north up the coast of British Columbia. It was a Hudson's Bay Company trading post too. Bellevue Farm was his first job as a manager. Griffin held the rank of "Chief Trader" and was a magistrate or judge for the island until late July 1859.

People who met him found him "very open and unreserved."

Griffin felt strongly about the right of Great Britain to claim the island. The Hudson's Bay Company had been there first. Still, after a bad start, he became friends with Henry Webber who had been sent to the island as a customs inspector for the Americans in 1854. Webber stayed a year, camping close to Bellevue Farm for protection from Indian raids. Oscar Olney took Webber's place. In 1856, Griffin heard that the northern Indians were looking for Olney. Griffin warned him and he was able to get away.

Griffin ran the Hudson's Bay Company Farm. He also acted as an agent of Britain. When Pickett brought troops to the island in July 1859, he wrote to Pickett expressing his displeasure. Griffin was later replaced by John De Courcy as magistrate, but continued to manage the farm.

Griffin saw the arrival of both the British marines and the American troops and the making of their camps. He continued to run the farm until 1862, then left. With so many Americans settling on the prairies, the farm no longer had enough acreage to make money. It is not known where Griffin went, but he possibly stayed with the Hudson's Bay Company.

The Pig in Question
Charles Griffin's Berkshire Boar

THE PIG IN QUESTION

The pig shot by Lyman Cutlar was most likely a **Berkshire**. The Berkshire is a breed of pig or hog that came to America from England in the 1800s. It is a medium-sized animal with straight ears and a short snout. It is generally black with some white markings. It doesn't have a lot of fat and is raised for meat —pork and bacon.

That Charles Griffin's Berkshire invaded Cutlar's potato patch should have come as no surprise. It was common practice during the 19th century to let pigs run outside a pen. They rooted in the woods and in the fields around the farm. As a result they became wild and hard to catch. If they wanted, they could run fast and did not look fat at all. In fact, they were often described as being "as thin as a rail." "Railback" was a common American name for such a pig. Only when they needed to be fattened up in the fall did the farmer need to catch them. He might tame them first by putting out apples or potato skins, which were a favorite. After they were caught, they were kept in pens and fed buttermilk and leftovers.

Farmers also kept a few pigs in pens. Pigs use their snouts to dig up the ground to get at roots. **Camus** and **wapato** are native Washington plants that have roots like carrots or tubers like potatoes. These would have been found on some of the prairies on San Juan Island. Farmers used the pig's ability to dig up things to clear his land. After tearing up the ground in its pen for several weeks, the pig and pen could be moved to a new spot. This was a good way to clear a garden.

Pigs were raised for meat like bacon and ham. There were no refrigerators back then, but it was easy to salt and smoke the meat. Smoked ham was prepared by covering the meat with salt. This dried out the meat. Then it was smoked, perhaps with alder wood. Pigs, even lean ones, were also an excellent source of **tallow**.

BELLEVUE DIARY

The prairie where Charles Grffin grazed his sheep.

Charles J. Griffin was the first manager of Bellevue Farm. His job was to run the farm. He kept a diary in his account book of daily life on the farm. He left around 1862. His first entries tell about how he built the farm and some of the troubles with the Americans. Look for how he spells the word "trespassing."

1854

April 2   John Ross and Time covering Beams in my house.

April 5   John Ross and Holland upper flooring my house.

April 6   John Ross and Holland commenced ceiling inside my house.

April 26	There is a report that the Americans have left Nisqually on two open boats well manned etc. to seize the Company's property on the Island here.
May 3	I paid them a visit without gleaning anything of importance.
June 7	John Ross commenced a stone foundation to my chimney.

1859

June 15	An American shot one of my pigs for tresspassing!!

Robert Firth took over Griffin's job in 1862. He kept a diary too. Later he would lease the farm and become a settler on the island. His diary tells us a lot about running a sheep "ranch." The sheep were grouped in flocks at several different "sheep stations." Sheep were sheared in early June, a practice still done today. Afterward, the sheep were dipped in tobacco juice. This killed any insects harmful to the sheep. Insects liked to lay their eggs on the animals. Today, sheep are dipped in chemicals made in factories. Notice how Firth spells "town", "tobacco", "shepherd", "plow" and "provisions." The words are underlined in his diary.

1865

Jan 13   Fine weather went to the Sheep Station.

Jan 15   Dick went to the sheep station with a
          fortnight provishans to the Sheephard.

Jan 17   Went to the new station after some pigs.

Feb 19   Went to towen with the cart for a
          barrel of fish.

Feb 24   Commenced to plough in the little fields.

Mar 11   Went to the lime kiln, found a sheep
          killed by dogs.

Apr 8   Planting potatoes.

Apr 19   Went to Victoria.

June 1   Fixing the barn for shearing

1866

June 8   Boiling tobaco.

June 12   Dipping sheep in tobaco

Victoria: Early Scenes

Victoria in the late 1850s.

Fort Victoria

BELLEVUE FARM (1853-1870)
(Photo by Lt. Richard Roche, RN)

BELLEVUE FARM (1853-1870)
(Photograph by Lt. Richard Roche, RN)

On December 13, 1853, the Hudson's Bay Company sent Charles J. Griffin to San Juan Island to set up Bellevue Sheep Farm. He arrived on the island with a large flock of sheep brought up from the Puget Sound Agricultural Company's Nisqually station in Washington Territory. On the southeastern end of the island on a grassy peninsula facing the Strait of Juan de Fuca, he set up his farm headquarters. It was about 100 yards from the shore. The following day, Griffin wrote his first entry into his account book. In it he wrote the number of livestock or animals on hand: 1,369 sheep, 1 horse, 1 stallion, 1 mare, 2 cows and calves, 1 heifer, 1 boar and 1 sow with young.

Eventually, one-story farm buildings made of hewn logs from trees cut down on the island were put up and by April of that year Griffin's own house was being built. A garden was put in and fences set up. Materials from Fort Victoria were brought over, including 2,000 bricks for a chimney and planks for the floor in the house. By the end of the year, most of his buildings were finished. Five years later, the farm would show "7 small houses, a barn, outhouse and shed." Six acres of land was being used for farming close to the buildings, but there were other places nearby where crops were grown. "Sheep stations" were set up at other points in the area a few miles away.

Bellevue Farm had workers from all over the world. There were two Englishmen, a Canadian, four Frenchmen, one Scotsman, several Indians and Kanakas (Hawaiians). To let the Americans know who the farm belonged to, Griffin put up a British flag.

The farm was active until 1864, but after American and English camps were set up, it lost money. American settlers moved into the abandoned sheep station buildings. After the islands were given to the United States in 1872, some of the buildings were moved to other parts of the island. The rest tumbled and fell down. Parts of a stone chimney are still visible at San Juan Island National Historic Park today.

Unit Three

The Cast Increases

THE CAST INCREASES

Lyman Cutlar shot the Hudson's Bay Company pig on June 15, 1859, but it wasn't until almost two weeks later that matters turned serious. At first it was just another island problem. In the six previous months, the number of Americans on the island had grown from one to twenty-five. They mainly settled on the prairies where the sheep runs were. American settlers typically did not like the Hudson's Bay Company because they could not compete with the big corporation's low prices. It angered them whenever they learned that an American had gone out of business. The Americans on the island were not certain what was said to Cutlar when the Hudson's Bay Company men from Fort Victoria visited him the day after he shot the pig, but they expected the worst. Cutlar told them he would be arrested for not paying a hundred dollars for the pig. To show their support, the Americans raised their flag on the Fourth of July. And when **Brigadier General William S. Harney** came up from Fort Vancouver, they told him an exaggerated version of the story and asked for the protection of soldiers. That's when the situation began to change from a list of complaints to a serious problem.

Harney was the commander of the U.S. Army Department of Oregon. He had been visiting on Vancouver Island with Governor Douglas. He told the settlers that they would have to write a **petition** or letter asking for help. The settlers did as he asked and signed it on July 11. They did not complain in the petition about the Hudson's Bay Company nor about the supposed threats to Cutlar. Instead they asked for protection against northern Indian raids. Years later one of the settlers confessed that Harney, seeking solid justification for what he was about to do, had coached them to do this. Seven days later, Harney ordered **Captain George Pickett** to bring Company D, 9th Infantry from Fort Bellingham. Pickett's orders were:

- ◆ Protect American citizens from the northern Indian raids.
- ◆ Resist British attempts to interfere in disputes between the Hudson's Bay Company and American citizens.

Harney also wrote orders for **Lieutenant Colonel Silas Casey**, the commander at Fort Steilacoom and Pickett's superior officer. Before long, the USS *Massachusetts*, a war steamer that carried troops and supplies around Puget Sound, was on its way to Bellingham Bay to pick up Pickett's men. It was a slow-moving boat, but it had eight 32-pound naval guns. When Pickett sailed from Fort Bellingham, he had 50 men on board. He anchored in Griffin Bay July 26, sending word to the American customs inspector Hubbs that he had arrived. The next day he placed his men on a hill just above the Hudson's Bay Company wharf on Griffin Bay. This hill was not only open and exposed to the wind, but also to potential enemy fire. Once his company was settled, Pickett posted a proclamation stating, in part, that the island was United States territory and no laws or courts other than those of the United States would be allowed or recognized. This alarmed Charles Griffin at Bellevue Farm and other British subjects who lived on the island. Later that day the first British warship arrived, the HMS *Satellite*. It was a modern, fast-moving ship with 21 guns.

MORE ACTORS ON THE STAGE

Sometimes what appear to be simple problems can mushroom into potential disasters. Before Pickett arrived with his soldiers, everyone seemed to know that trouble was brewing on San Juan Island. People talked about it in the newspapers both in Fort Victoria and in the American settlements around Puget Sound. When it did happen, some treated the landing of troops as a holiday event. People sailed or rowed over to take a look. However, some took it very seriously, especially men such as Governor Douglas and General Harney. Neither liked the other's country very much. Douglas thought the Americans wanted to grab all of the land. He believed Harney wanted to be president of the United States and was looking to commit an act that would make him a hero. He also believed that George Pickett was no better than a trespasser. On the other hand, Harney viewed Douglas as another grasping Hudson's Bay Company man who, with the blessing of the crown, was prepared to evict American citizens from the islands even though the boundary question was far from settled. Unfortunately, these hot-headed individuals were in positions that made the situation far more dangerous than it should have been. It would take cooler heads to prevent war from breaking out. One of these cooler heads belonged to **Geoffrey Phipps Hornby**, captain of the HMS *Tribune*, a British steam frigate of 31 guns.

On July 29, Hornby sailed into Griffin Bay and anchored the *Tribune* so that her guns pointed at Pickett's camp. The *Satellite* had left the day before to search for the U.S. Boundary Commissioner, Archibald Campbell. With him were 235 sailors and 23 Royal Marines. He had been ordered by Douglas "to prevent the landing of further armed parties of U.S. soldiers for the purpose of occupation." Douglas had the power to do this because when **Admiral R.L. Baynes**, the commander of the British forces in the Pacific area, was away, Douglas, as vice-admiral, was in charge. Hornby and Pickett met a couple of times to attempt a solution. Pickett was clearly outnumbered, but Hornby knew that the 50 American soldiers could be joined by half again as many local settlers. If fired upon, the Americans could scatter and "take to the bush" and then perhaps do harm to the cattle at Bellevue Farm. Worse, if British Royal Marines were to land, Hornby feared there would be bloodshed. Four days later the *Satellite* returned along with the HMS *Plumper*, both of which brought more marines. They also brought new orders from Douglas. Hornby was to land troops by nightfall and occupy San Juan Island along with the Americans. However, Hornby knew that Pickett would not allow that to happen. After visiting Pickett to tell him about his orders, Hornby returned to his ship to think. He decided to disobey Douglas' orders.

Hornby made a courageous decision. Sometimes making the right choice can be a painful experience. Hornby knew that there would be some who would be angry with him—especially Douglas—but he also knew that it was foolish for his country to go to war against the Americans over a group of small islands in a far corner of the world. A boundary commission had been appointed to settle who owned the islands. So Hornby waited, believing that his superior officer, Admiral Baynes, would support him. In the end, he was right. And there were others who felt the same way, even though the Americans continued to build fortifications and increased the number of soldiers on the island to nearly 500. The British captains at the Esquimalt naval anchorage on Vancouver Island, anticipating how Admiral Baynes would react to the governor's decision, also did not think that it was wise to land troops. Sure enough, when Baynes returned to Vancouver Island on August 5, he canceled Douglas' orders. They would wait until they heard from London—even if it took a month or longer.

SETTLING ARGUMENTS: ROLE PLAYING

The Cast

NAME / COUNTRY	WHAT THEY BELIEVED
General William S. Harney, United States	San Juan Islands belonged to the U.S. British laws and courts did not apply to American citizens. The island and American citizens would be defended against the British. Stretched the truth.
Governor James Douglas, Great Britain	San Juan Island belonged to Great Britain. Thought the Americans wanted not only the San Juan Islands, but Vancouver Island and lands north of the 49th parallel.
Captain George Pickett, United States	The island must be defended against any British troops landing. Only American laws applied to Americans. They would fight against all odds to protect American interests.
Captain Geoffrey Hornby, Great Britain	Great Britain could afford to wait. It had superior forces. Did not want to ruin the country's reputation by fighting over something neither country could claim.
General Winfield Scott, United States	The crisis could be settled without fighting. A military joint occupation was the best solution until arbitration decided who owned the islands.
Rear Admiral R. L. Baynes, Great Britain	Experienced and calm. Felt that negotiation was the best solution, though Royal Navy could certainly do a lot of damage to American forces. Island not worth fighting over, even if the British won.

Conflict is another name for an argument. Often when people are in conflict, they don't admit their feelings. They may choose to ignore the problem or simply walk away. Other people get angry and use abusive language or start hitting. At its worst, conflict can turn into war. The angry parties believe there must be a winner and a loser. **And each will do whatever is needed to ensure they are the winner.** A confrontation or fight prevents cooperation and peaceful problem solving. Some examples of **confrontation:**

- ◆ fighting
- ◆ threatening someone

The main characters in the Pig War were definitely in conflict. Douglas thought he was right and Harney and Pickett thought they were right. Pickett was willing to stand up to the greatest naval force in the world at the time, along with their guns and marines. Douglas wanted the British naval officers to help land the Royal Marines and if there was a battle, blow the Americans off the hill with their powerful guns. Fortunately, there were men on both sides of the conflict who thought otherwise.

When there is a conflict, one possible answer is to **communicate**. Communication is a form of problem solving. People try to cooperate and understand each other. They look for solutions that meet both sides' needs. Communicating with each side can yield an outcome satisfying to both, a solution in which everyone wins. Some examples of **communication:**

- ◆ trying to understand the other person's point of view
- ◆ talking openly about the problem
- ◆ trying to come up with a solution that makes both people happy

Communicating also involves **listening**. To be an active listener you can:

- ◆ put yourself in the other person's place
- ◆ show understanding by your tone of voice, eye contact, facial expressions
- ◆ listen without interrupting, giving suggestions or advice
- ◆ retell the other person's important thoughts and feelings

Using these communication and active listening ideas, role play the disagreement between the British and Americans. Use Harney and Douglas (or Douglas and Pickett) as the main **antagonists** or opponents. Use Hornby or Winfield Scott as an **arbitrator** or referee in the conflict. (See "The Cast" sheet and what they believed.) How would they settle the argument using these conflict resolution ideas and the information from the chart? Would it sound differently from what happened in history? Make props for the characters. Douglas might have a big bow tie and jacket; General Harney an army

July 28, 1859

EXTRA! EXTRA READ ALL ABOUT IT!

We suppose our neighbors may grumble a little at this summary way of settling the disputed title, but then it is the privilege of John Bull to grumble and the motley crowd of native born British subjects congregated in those new Colonies may grumble away.

Pioneer and
Democrat,
Olympia,
Washington
Territory

July 29, 1859

We learn that a company of U.S. soldiers under command of Capt. Pickett, were expected to land at San Juan Island yesterday, from Semiahmoo, in order to erect barracks and fortifications. They were ordered there by Gen. Harney, when up here a short time ago. We trust our government will call our insatiable neighbor to account for the unwarrantable assumption.

Colonist,
Victoria, Colony
of Vancouver
Island

CAPTAIN GEORGE E. PICKETT
Commander of Camp Pickett

GEORGE E. PICKETT
Commander of Camp Pickett
July 27, 1859 to August 10, 1859
April 28, 1860 to July 25, 1861

Born January 28, 1825, in Virginia.

Went to West Point Military Academy and graduated last in his class in 1846. Served in the Mexican War 1846-1847 and was a garrison officer in Texas 1849-1855. Promoted to captain in 1855.

Established Fort Bellingham in 1856 in Whatcom County, Washinton Territory, to protect against the northern Indians.

Married Indian woman from the "northern Indians." Son put into the care of a family in Olympia, Washington, after his mother died.

Ordered to occupy San Juan Island on July 27, 1859, to protect American citizens from the northern tribes. Company D, 9th Infantry consisted of 50 enlisted men, or soldiers who signed up, and 4 officers. Took orders seriously.

Relieved of command on August 10, 1859; reinstated in April 1860. During his command dealt with many problems of settlers. Brought order to the community outside the camp.

Reported to the Confederate Army in the fall of 1861. Promoted to brigadier general in January 1862 and major general in September 1862.

Led fatal charge at Battle of Gettysburg during the Civil War. Almost lost his entire command at the Battle of Five Forks (1865), which led directly to the Southern surrender at Appomattox.

Fled the country for war crimes. Charges dropped with the help of General Grant. Moved to Richmond, Virginia, where he sold insurance.
Died July 30, 1875.

JAMES DOUGLAS
Governor of British Columbia
and
Royal Crown Colony of Vancouver Island

JAMES DOUGLAS
Governor of British Columbia
and
Royal Crown Colony of Vancouver Island

Born in the Caribbean in 1803. Scottish parentage.

Came to North America in 1816 and worked with Northwest Company in 1819. Worked with their trading post until the company joined with Hudson's Bay Company.

Went to Fort Vancouver in 1831 and rose to assistant post factor under John McLoughlin.

Founded Fort Victoria in 1843, then became factor at Fort Vancouver in 1847.

Became chief factor at Fort Victoria in 1849.

Appointed governor of Crown Colony of Vancouver Island on August 26, 1851. Later became governor of Crown Colony of British Columbia in 1859. Held both posts until his retirement in 1864.

Considered the San Juans "a dependency of Vancouver's Island." San Juan Island had been claimed a year before the Treaty of Oregon (1846) by placing an engraved wooden tablet on Mt. Finlayson on San Juan Island. Didn't like Americans settling anywhere near the islands.

Was vice-admiral of Pacific fleet when Admiral Baynes was away.

After Pickett landed, sent orders on July 27 stating that land belonging to the Hudson's Bay Company should be returned to it; that trespassers (American settlers) should be arrested and brought to Victoria for a court hearing; naval and military force should be used, if necessary.

WILLIAM S. HARNEY
Commander
U.S. Army Department of Oregon
1858-1860

WILLIAM S. HARNEY
Commander
U.S. Army Department of Oregon
1858-1860

Born August 27, 1800, in Haysboro, Tennessee.

Commissioned a second lieutenant in 1818.

Served in several Indian campaigns and the Mexican War before San Juan Island incident. Served under General Winfield Scott. Did not have good relationship with Winfield Scott, who thought him "impetuous and unmanageable." He did things without thinking and didn't take orders very well.

Became the first commander of the newly formed Department of Oregon in 1858. His headquarters were at Fort Vancouver on the Columbia River. He was in charge of military posts in northern Oregon and Washington Territory, which contained Idaho and western Montana too. Did not like the British.

Following the shooting of the pig, ordered Pickett to take Company D, 9th Infantry to San Juan Island on July 18, 1859, to "protect settlers against northern Indians." Also sent Captain Haller with Company I, 4th Infantry. The sending of troops made a minor problem a big problem. Failed to consult with Archibald Campbell who was the U.S. civilian authority in charge of boundary negotiations with Britain.

Rejected the idea of joint occupancy and on August 6 ordered more troops to the island.

In September 1859, Acting Secretary of State sent letter: "The President was not prepared to learn that you ordered military possession to be taken of the island of San Juan."

Recalled from Washington Territory June 8, 1860. Served in the Union Army in Missouri during Civil War. Removed from command in 1861. Was an Indian commissioner after the war.

Died May 9, 1889.

SILAS CASEY
Commander of Camp Pickett
August 10 to October 18, 1859

SILAS CASEY
Commander of Camp Pickett
August 10 to October 18, 1859

Born July 12, 1807, in Rhode Island.

Graduated from West Point in 1826 near the bottom of his class.

Served in Florida and Mexican War.

Deputy Commander of the 9th Infantry at Fort Steilacoom from January 1856 to August 1861.

Ordered by Harney to help Pickett and take command of San Juan Island on August 6, 1859. He was also to take heavy guns from the ship *Massachusetts* and use them to defend the island.

Selected final site of American Camp.

Recalled from the Northwest at beginning of the Civil War. Reached the rank of major general of volunteers in 1862. Prepared a manual of infantry tactics, Casey's Tactics, used by both the North and the South.

Retired as colonel of 4th Infantry in 1868.

Died in 1882.

CAPTAIN GEOFFREY PHIPPS HORNBY
HMS *TRIBUNE*

CAPTAIN GEOFFREY PHIPPS HORNBY
HMS *TRIBUNE*

Born in 1825 in England, the son of Admiral Sir Phipps Hornby.

Described as "tall, slightly-built, quiet, firm, with chestnut hair and hazel eyes."

Joined the Royal Navy when he was 12 years of age. At 21, father appointed Commander in Chief, Pacific Station. Hornby served under his father as flag lieutenant.

In 1850, promoted to captain.

HMS *Tribune* was his first independent command. Took over in Hong Kong in October 1858. Arrived at Esquimalt in February 1859 after dangerous Pacific crossing. Forty of his crew deserted immediately.

Sent to San Juan Island on July 29, 1859, at 5 p.m., arriving in Griffin Bay at 9 p.m.

Disobeyed Douglas' orders to land troops; he and others felt that the governor had gone beyond his authority.

Left Esquimalt for England in 1860.

Had brilliant career. Became one of the Sea Lords, an important position. Later knighted by Queen Victoria. Considered the Royal Navy's foremost expert on tactical warfare.

Died in 1895.

ROBERT LAMBERT BAYNES
Admiral, RN, Commander, Pacific Station

ROBERT LAMBERT BAYNES
Admiral

Born in Scotland.

Entered Royal Navy in 1810. During the War of 1812, he served at the siege of New Orleans. Became captain in 1828 and rear admiral in 1855.

Took command of Pacific Station in 1858. Later became a vice-admiral.

Described as a "well-controlled man, a counterbalance to emotional Douglas." Plain, little, with a big-heart. "Full of salt and fresh fun."

Knighted for his role in the Pig War crisis.

Died about 1869.

GENERAL WINFIELD SCOTT
Commander in Chief of United States Army

GENERAL WINFIELD SCOTT
Commander in Chief of United States Army

Born on June 13, 1786, on a plantation near Petersburg, Virginia.

Was a lawyer for a few years, then in 1808 joined the Army as a captain.

Known as "Old Fuss and Feathers" for his formality in dress and behavior, but also called the Great Pacifier.

Fought in the War of 1812 and was a hero of the Mexican War.

Was the Whig candidate for president of the United States in 1852, but lost.

Was mediator in the Aroostook War, an international boundary dispute between Maine and New Brunswick settlers. Was asked to resolve the crisis at San Juan Island in September 1859.

Detested Harney, whom he thought was a favorite of Democratic presidents. Had early problems with him in wars in Florida and Mexico.

Felt that a joint civil occupation of the island was not possible and advocated a joint military occupation. Agreed with Douglas to remove reinforcements until governments could decide how to proceed. British finally agreed to joint military occupation in January 1860.

Scott was commander in chief of the army at the outbreak of the Civil War. Served for a short time, then retired at 75 years of age.

Died on May 29, 1866.

HENRY MARTYN ROBERT
U.S. Army Corps of Engineers

HENRY MARTYN ROBERT
U.S. Army Corps of Engineers

Born in South Carolina.

Graduated from West Point in 1857, fourth in his class.

Spent entire career in the Corps of Engineers. Stayed with the North during the Civil War.

Built a redoubt for the 32-pound cannons for Camp Pickett. Never finished because of joint occupancy agreement. Redoubt was known as Robert's Gopher Hole.

Became Chief of Engineers with the rank of brigadier general in 1901.

Best known for his Robert's Rules of Order, which is used in all meetings. Said to have written the book after attending a meeting of settlers on San Juan Island where everyone was shouting out of order.

Died in 1923.

HORNBY WRITES HIS WIFE IN ENGLAND
July 31, 1859

[San Juan Island] is the one that lies nearest Vancouver's and has always been held by the Hudson Bay Co. as a sheep-farm, and the agent has until lately had a commission as a magistrate. The Americans claim the island, and...a hot-headed general Hearney [sic] (who hopes to get his name up for a future President) has sent a small detachment of soldiers who have formed a camp on the island and hoisted their flag. Now, the Governor's instructions expressly tell him we are to commit no act of war, and we are not allowed to bundle these fellows off neck and crop, so he takes a medium course. He sends over a magistrate, who is to take legal steps to warn them off the land...

Everything has changed since I began my letter.... I have received fresh orders to take no steps against these men at present, or prevent others landing. We have sent for a detachment of marines....The object now seems to be to avoid a collision at all hazards.

December 4, 1859

I hear that Governor Douglas has got much praise in England for keeping peace with the Yankees. That is rather good, when one knows that he would hear nothing but shooting them all at first and that, after all, peace was only preserved by my not complying with his wishes, as I felt he was all wrong from the first. I got the abuse for saying that San Juan was not more our island than the Americans; and that we should be equally wrong in landing troops there and now they find out I was right.

LETTERS OF GRIFFIN AND PICKETT

July 30, 1859

Sir: I have the honor to inform you that the island of San Juan on which your camp is pitched, is the property and in the occupation of Hudson's Bay Company, and to request that you and the whole of the party who have landed from the American vessels will immediately cease to occupy the same. Should you be unwilling to comply with my request, I feel bound to apply to the civil authorities. Awaiting your reply, I have the honor to be, sir, your obedient servant.

CHAS. JNO. GRIFFIN

July 30, 1859

Sir: Your communication of this instant has been received. I have to state that I do not acknowledge the right of the Hudson's Bay Company to dictate my course of action. I am here by virtue of an order from my government, and shall remain till recalled by the same authority.

I am, Sir, very respectfully, your obedient servant.

GEORGE E. PICKETT

Unit Four

Finding a Solution

FINDING A SOLUTION

Throughout August while the British waited for their government's answer to the crisis, Harney and Douglas exchanged letters. Pickett had been replaced on August 10 by Lieutenant Colonel Silas Casey, who continued to build up fortifications on a hilltop overlooking Griffin Bay and the Strait of Juan de Fuca. He moved his men for a final time on August 22 and set up American Camp in its present-day position. The *Tribune* and the other British warships continued to anchor in the bay below, but no troops were landed. Both countries sent justices to take care of people breaking the law. And it is said that Cutlar was arrested by American constables— men in charge of keeping the peace— put on trial, and fined for the loss of the Hudson's Bay Company pig. There is, however, no record of this happening. What was happening was that tourists were coming to the island to visit Pickett's camp. British officers from the ships, in turn, often entertained the Americans. No one was certain what would happen, but by summer's end news of Harney's actions appeared in newspapers from San Francisco to New York. For the first time, the President of the United States learned about Harney's invasion of San Juan Island and he was not pleased. On September 19, **Lieutenant General Winfield Scott**, commander of the U.S. Army, left his headquarters in New York City for the Pacific Northwest to take charge of the situation. By now officials from both governments in London and Washington City (Washington D.C.) were working together to end the crisis. The Americans assured the British that they would reduce the American command on the island to one company. However, because of the vast distance involved, it required nearly six weeks for word to reach Washington, D.C.; no one in Washington or London yet knew if fighting had taken place.

Scott arrived on the Columbia River on the evening of October 20, 1859, and steamed up to Harney's headquarters near Fort Vancouver. An aide was sent over at two in the morning to inform Harney that Scott had arrived. It didn't take long for Scott to let Harney know how the president felt about the crisis. It was going to end. The United States was going to propose a joint military occupation. Harney sputtered that a joint occupancy would be a disgrace to the country. The seventy-three year old general got up and criticized Harney sharply. Harney left shaken. They never saw each other again during Scott's stay in the Pacific Northwest. Scott traveled to Fort Townsend at the mouth of the Puget Sound and quickly moved to contact Governor Douglas about a joint military occupation. Douglas suggested a civil occupation, but Scott thought a military one was better because it would be difficult for judges and magistrates to keep the peace in neutral territory while maintaining international harmony. A military occupation also would discourage northern Indians from harming settlers on the island— American and British.

Scott and Douglas never did agree to a joint military occupation. However, they did agree to reduce the numbers of their respective forces on the island and anchored in Griffin Bay while Douglas awaited word from his government. That word came in January 1860 when the British government authorized a joint military occupation. The agreement called for the number of troops to be reduced to no more than a hundred men for each nation. In addition, to prevent any settler from switching sides to escape being charged with disobeying the law, anyone disturbing the peace would be turned over to their nearest national authority for "instant removal" from the island. If the lawbreaker showed up a second time and tried to change citizenship, the opposite commander could kick him off the island. Law and order had arrived.

SETTLING ARGUMENTS: GETTING THE MESSAGE

One of the most important parts of settling an argument is communication. If it is a problem close to home or in a classroom, talking to someone is easy. When it involves governments thousands of miles away, the problem becomes more difficult.

The governments of Great Britain and the United States definitely had a problem in 1859 because the Pacific Northwest was so isolated. There were no telephones and "rapid" transportation was limited to steam boats and horseback. Messages from the San Juan Islands to London or Washington City went by courier on an ocean steamer to Panama where the messenger got on a train, crossed the isthmus to the Atlantic Ocean side and boarded another steamer for London or New York. In the early days before a trans-isthmus railroad was built, it could be a deadly trip. Yellow fever, which was carried by mosquitos, killed hundreds of travelers passing through Panama. Overall, the trip to Washington took about six weeks. This lack of rapid communication made settling the crisis more difficult. For example, the crisis on San Juan Island began on July 27, but the President didn't learn of it until September 2. The president contacted Lord Lyons, the British ambassador in Washington City, who, in turn, sent a telegram to Quebec City in Canada. The colonial government there then sent it to London by ship. The ship arrived in London on September 29, two weeks after the message was sent from Quebec.

Today, disasters are reported within seconds by cell phone or by calling 911. Governments also can contact each other anywhere in the world through satellite links. Communication is very fast.

Getting the Message

Step one: Divide the class into two groups. Divide each group into three teams. Each team will write a message. They can:

Describe the Pig War crisis and in words tell where the Americans and British are located.

Make up their own problem. Describe in words where the problem is located. For example, your classroom has run out of pencils. You need to send someone to get more from the school office or where supplies are kept. Give directions on how to get there.

Step Two: Trade messages with another team in the group. Read what the message says, then draw a picture of what was said. When everyone is done, pass the picture to a new team in the group.

Step Three: Using the information in the picture, write in words what problem is shown in the message. Is it clear? Does it read like the original message?

Project of a Temporary Settlement, &c.

WHEREAS the island of San Juan, in dispute between the governments of the United States and Great Britain, is now occupied by a detachment of United States troops, protection against Indian incursions having been petitioned for by American citizens, resident thereon, and against such occupation a formal protest has been entered on behalf of Her Britannic majesty's government by His excellency James Douglas, esquire, C.B. Governor of the Colony of Vancouver's Island and its Dependencies, and Vice-admiral of the same—

It is now proposed by Lieutenant General Scott, Commander in Chief of the Army of the United States on behalf of his government, and in deference to the great interests of the two nations, that a joint occupancy be substituted for the present one, which proposition being accepted by His Excellency, it is hereby stipulated and agreed between the said Scott and the said Douglas that the substitution without prejudice to the claim of either government to the sovereignty of the entire island, and until that question shall be amicably settled, shall consist of two detachments of infantry, riflemen, or marines of the two nations, neither detachment of more than one hundred men, with their appropriate arms only, and to be posted in separate camps...

Unit Five

Keeping
the Peace

KEEPING THE PEACE 1859-1872

American Camp was started in the summer of 1859 and would go through several names—among them Camp Pickett, Camp San Juan and Camp Steele. English Camp came into being on March 21, 1860, with the arrival of a company of the British Royal Marine Light Infantry at Garrison Bay on the northern end of San Juan Island. Within days, trees were cleared and an extensive building program was begun. Typically, the British first planted a vegetable garden, which later became a formal affair. The Royal Marine camp would be called the "British Camp" by the British. But to San Juan Islanders it has always been "English Camp."

From the beginning, the camps offered high contrasts. American Camp was built, in part, from boards taken from old Fort Bellingham and would always be in a state of neglect. Washington City was thousands of miles away and San Juan Island was remote. The command there was often forgotten, especially during the Civil War years. English Camp, on the other hand, was close to Victoria and Royal Navy carpenters and supplies. The camp was set in a very pretty place and the officers who served there built charming homes much like those they had in posts around the world. Groups would come over from Victoria for the day and picnic. There were concerts.

Relations between the camps were very friendly, with the officers getting together frequently for dinner or outings. There were celebrations of national holidays: Fourth of July for the Americans, Queen Victoria's Birthday on May 24 for the British. At Christmas and New Year's both camps gave parties for the settlers and each other. There were even horse races. At a race in June 1860, the black mare of Charles Griffin of Hudson's Bay Company won the sweepstakes. A military road was built between the camps so that the soldiers and marines could exchange visits. Once the matter of joint occupation was settled upon, things went very well and for 12 years there was peace between the camps and the nations.

Life at American Camp was much like life in any U.S. Army camp on the frontier: ordered and regimented with occasional "leave" or time off. Since the officers made more money than the regular soldiers, they had more opportunities to leave the island and go to the settlements of Olympia, Port Townsend, Victoria on Vancouver Island or to Whatcom on Bellingham Bay. Some were able to leave the Puget Sound area altogether. The common soldiers were not so fortunate. They spent their days off visiting with local settlers on the island, going hunting and, occasionally, getting in trouble at San Juan Village, which appeared on the island within days after Captain Pickett landed with Company D. Some men arrived and set up tents and ramshackle buildings at the water's edge and began selling a variety of goods, including whiskey. For the next 12 years that item would cause headaches with every commander at Camp Pickett. Despite the fact that British warships were in the bay training their guns on Pickett's camp, the rowdy little community thrived. It was to be the only civilian settlement on the island until the army camp closed in 1874. That was when village residents began drifting over to the new town of Friday Harbor about five miles north. In 1890, the virtually deserted San Juan Village burned to the ground.

English Camp was a much more comfortable place to live—it wasn't as exposed to lashing winds as was American Camp. If there were complaints about buildings or living conditions, they could be addressed soon enough. The Royal Navy's Pacific Station headquarters was in Esquimalt, just across the Haro Strait, not in far-off Washington City. Life at English Camp also was orderly and regimented, and while alcohol was consumed in great quantities, it was not as big a problem for the British as it was for the Americans. However, the marines also got into trouble and rebelled at military life, sometimes deserting or running away from the camp to look for gold in British Columbia or land in Washington Territory where they one day hoped to homestead.

The joint military occupation of San Juan Island lasted 12 years. It came to an end in the fall of 1872 when news arrived that the United States had been awarded the San Juan Islands by an international mediator. On November 18, **Captain William Addis Delacombe**, commander at English Camp, was ordered to withdraw the Royal Marines to Vancouver Island. At sunset on November 21, the British flag was lowered for the last time at the camp. The next day, the marines left. Worried that the buildings at the camp would be taken over by American settlers, Delacombe remained on shore until the camp was turned over to the last commander of American Camp, **First Lieutenant James A. Haughey**. On November 24, Haughey sent **Second Lieutenant Fred Epstein** to receive the buildings from the British. Bringing an American flag with him, Epstein was disappointed to find the British flagpole chopped down. He was told that it was to be used as a spar on a ship which had lost its mast in a Pacific crossing.

Both camps were occupied by American troops until 1874 when the camps were closed and the soldiers were withdrawn to Fort Townsend. In a short time, the property was claimed by settlers and the buildings sold at auction to the highest bidders. Some were occupied on site, while others were moved elsewhere on the island. The military use of the camps had finally come to an end.

SETTLING ARGUMENTS: KEEPING THE PEACE

Settling an argument may seem the end to an event, but often it is the beginning. How are people now going to get along? Are there any rules? Surprisingly, it takes a lot of work to make peace.

One of the issues facing both sides was the matter of law enforcement. Since the island could not be claimed by either the United States or Great Britain, both American and British subjects were wondering who to turn to if a law was broken. Would a British subject be arrested only by a British peace officer? Would it be the same for an American? Who would decide? Those who broke the law often left the island and claimed that they were a citizen of the other country. They would protest their treatment.

In the early months of the military occupation, law enforcement problems often were handled by the army under the supervision of **Captain Lewis Cass Hunt** of Company C, 4th Infantry, who had replaced Captain Pickett. This infuriated the liquor sellers and other residents of San Juan Village. After Hunt shut down some of the "whiskey ranches," a petition was sent to the governor of Washington Territory. Hunt was removed and replaced by Pickett in April 1860, but Pickett was no friend to them either. He also punished whiskey sellers and even investigated a murder. When English Camp opened in the spring of 1860, the British commander joined Pickett in disciplining lawbreakers.

Eventually, it was accepted that post commanders from both military camps had the supreme authority on the island. In 1865, a law reduced the number of stores on the island to two—one on each end of the island—which ended a number of the illegal businesses. Both commanders worked together to take care of problems that arose from a joint military occupation. Settlers could complain, but until the boundary decision was settled, it was the best solution.

Rules of the Game

Think of a game such as **Red Light, Green Light** (running and stopping on command) that has penalties when a player is caught. On the blackboard write:

* What happens when the leader or the person who is "It" discovers that a rule has been broken?
* What is the penalty?
* Is there more than one penalty?

Fill in the answers, then think about this idea: What if there are two leaders for the game, but each leader knows different rules from playing at a different school? Like the British and American commanders, the leaders may have to decide which penalty is best. The players will then have to agree to the penalty, even if they know the other school's rules.

MILITARY CAMP LIFE
1859-1872

TYPICAL DAY AT CAMP PICKETT
THE DAILY ALTA CALIFORNIA, NOVEMBER 4, 1859

This news account was made during the last week of the crisis, just days before General Scott visited Griffin Bay where all the British and American vessels were anchored. The Americans still had quite a large number of troops and Lieutenant Robert was still working on the redoubt. After Scott left, the troops were reduced to one company and the redoubt was abandoned. This account of daily life shows a side of army life that would continue for the next twelve years.

"The reveille is beated at 5 ½ o'clock—and the fifes, drums and trumpets keep up a general hub-bub for nigh an hour. The men breakfast, but the major portion of the officers content themselves with a hot cup of coffee and a slice of toast. At eight o'clock there is a general battalion drill. The martial music sounds and each company with its officer or officers come upon the ground in double quick time—late regulations, or "Shanghae" step—at which the members of the force are peculiar adept. Drill over, the men divest themselves of their new uniforms, and repair to their various labors: some to guard duty and others to special detail; detachments from each company to the redoubt; artillerists to the placing of their guns and experiments at elevation and depression; cooks to their messes; carpenters, bricklayers and tailors to their work; detachments to cutting fuel; the inmates of the guardhouse, of whom there are quite a number, to various menial duties, cleaning the ground of stumps, aided by oxen, cleaning up or working at the trenches... Tattoo beats at eight o'clock. The officers receive and pay visits from and to the frigate SATELLITE. They have mess dinners on land and sea—the former under the stars and stripes and the latter under the British jack. A familiar chat around the bright wood fire or a quick rubber of whist manages to kill time; and sleep to those not on guard duty soon leaves the camp to the solitude of the guard, only to be broken by the visits of (Native women), of whom quite a number are on the Island. These, with liqueur selling, are the only troubles which beset the officers."

AMERICAN CAMP
1859-1874

AMERICAN CAMP
1859-1874

Established on July 27, 1859, at Griffin Bay by Captain George Pickett. The camp had 50 soldiers and 3 officers of Company D, 9th Infantry.

"The Americans have formed a camp 200 yards from the beach with two howitzers. The ground rises considerably behind the camp and on either side of the 300 yards flanked by woods."—Captain Hornby, July 29, 1859.

On August 1, Pickett moved his troops to the opposite side of the peninsula near a spring Griffin used for his sheep. The new location was out of range of the HMS *Tribune*, a British steam frigate with 31 guns.

August 10, after Colonel Casey landed, the present site was chosen.

August 22, 450 men relocated to the north slope of a ridge just north of the Hudson's Bay Company barns. The soldiers lived in Sibley tents for several months, but it appears that Pickett's Company D lived in buildings from Fort Bellingham, which had been taken down and brought over on a steamer. New buildings were also built. When he left in December, an enlisted men's quarters, laundresses' quarters, mess room and kitchen were in use.

A four-square-mile military reserve was set up in December 1859 to keep whiskey peddlers away from the camp.

The camp had several names— Camp San Juan, Camp Pickett, Camp Steele— and several commanders, some with families.

During the Civil War, there was little construction. After the war, repairs were needed.

Closed on July 17, 1874, the buildings were moved elsewhere or used by settler families for their homesteads.

AMERICAN CAMP
1859

AMERICAN CAMP
1859

This early photo shows the encampment at its present-day site.

Soldiers were living in tents. Not all the trees had been cleared from the parade ground. Soldiers dressed up in regulation dress uniforms so they would look as impressive as the British.

What else do you see about camp life?

ENGLISH CAMP
(ROYAL MARINE CAMP)
1860-1872

ENGLISH CAMP
(ROYAL MARINE CAMP)
1860-1872

This camp was established March 21, 1860.

It was first surveyed as a site in the winter of 1859. It sloped "gently to the S.W.," was "well-sheltered with a good supply of water..." Behind it was a trail to the Hudson's Bay farm. The site was on Garrison Bay at the northwest end of the island.

The Royal Marines landed and set up camp. Admiral Baynes ordered building materials for a store house, cook stoves and a five-oared whale boat immediately. Men lived in tents.

In August, Admiral Baynes ordered winter quarters built for the marines.

CAMP LIFE

CAMP LIFE

Until permanent camps were set up, the soldiers at American Camp lived in tents. The tents were called Sibley tents after the man who designed them. Each could hold about twenty men and were heated by a sheet iron stove. Later, the soldiers lived in wooden barracks. American Camp had only recently been moved to its permanent location when this photograph was taken by a Royal Navy officer.

SCHEDULE

Reveille	6:30 AM
Breakfast	7:00 AM
Fatigue	7:30 AM
Sick Call	8:00 AM
Guard Mount	9:00 AM
Drill	10:00 AM
Recall from Drill	11:00 AM
Dinner	Noon
Fatigue	1:00 PM
Recall from Fatigue	5:00 PM

THE CHOW LINE

THE CHOW LINE

This lithograph shows a typical **chow line** or food line. Being the army, it was orderly. Notice that the men have brought a variety of containers to hold their hot food. When American Camp was first set up, the soldiers were given rations, but eventually a mess hall and bakery were built.

Breakfast was served at 7:00 and dinner at noon. What time of day do you eat?

Behind them, you can see the camp stretching out on the hills. Although American Camp did not look exactly like this, it does show the layout of a military camp which would be very similar.

DAILY SOLDIER'S RATION
(Camp)

12 oz. of PORK OR BACON
Or
1 lb. 4 oz. SALT OR FRESH BEEF

1 lb. 6 oz. of SOFT BREAD or FLOUR
Or
1 lb. of HARD BREAD

Or
1 lb. 4 oz. of CORN MEAL

...with every 100 rations:

1 peck of BEANS or PEAS

10 lbs. GREEN COFFEE
or 8 lbs. ROASTED and GROUND
or 1 lb. 8 oz. of TEA

15 lbs. of SUGAR

2 qts. of SALT

4 qts. of VINEGAR

4 oz. PEPPER

1 qt. of MOLASSES

1 lb. 4 oz. of CANDLES

4 lbs. of SOAP

Hardtack

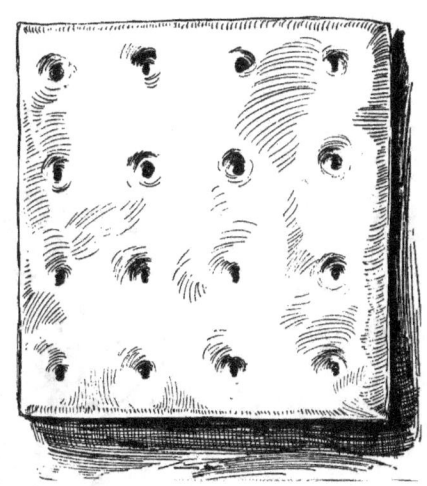

" 'Tis the song of the soldier, weary, hungry, and faint,

Hard tack, hard tack, come again no more."

One of the most important rations given to the soldier on a daily basis was **hard bread** or as it was called during the Civil War, "**hardtack.**" It was a two-by-three inch square "plain flour-and-water biscuit." It was baked in Baltimore on the east coast, boxed up and shipped out to American Camp by boat, a journey of 5 weeks. There it was distributed in batches of nines and tens.

As a food it was a healthy part of the soldier's diet, but three conditions could make it one of the worst items on the menu:

1. Baked so hard that they could not be bitten.

2. Became moldy or wet after being boxed up too soon after baking or from being out in the weather.

3. Became infested with maggots and weevils during storage.

As a rule, hardtack that was wet was thrown out, but hardtack with weevils was eaten. In the dark, it was hard to tell if they were there.

WAYS OF PREPARING

- Eat it plain or crumbled in the coffee.
- Used as a thickener in soups.
- Crumbled in cold water, then fried in fat in a pan.
- Roasted on a split stick.

Hardtack Recipe

Hardtack Recipe

Students can get a taste of soldier life by making their own hardtack. The following "receipt" or recipe is based on an 1862 U.S. Army book of recipes. For this recipie you will need:

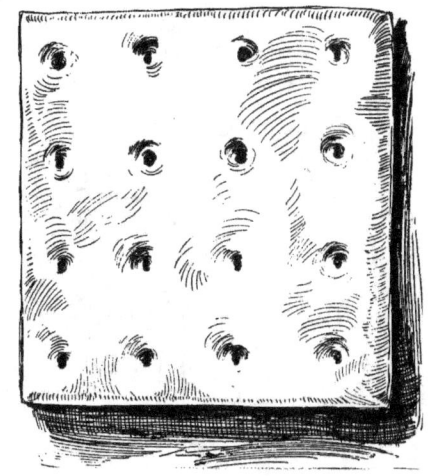

5 cups Flour (unbleached)
1 Tablespoon Baking Powder
1 Tablespoon Salt
1-1/4 cups of Water
A mixing bowl
Scraper

A greased cookie sheet

Preheat the oven to 450 degrees F. In a mixing bowl, combine the ingredients to make a stiff, but not dry dough. The dough should be elastic, not sticky.

Take the mound of dough and flatten it onto a greased cookie sheet and roll the dough into a flat shape about 1/2 inch thick.

Using a bread knife, divide the dough into 3x3 squares. Then take a clean 10-penny nail and poke a grid of holes across the face of each 3x3 square.

Bake in the oven for 20 minutes or until lightly browned. Take out and cool.

The hardtack will be soft at first, but after a day or two will become hard.

A U.S. Soldier's Clothing

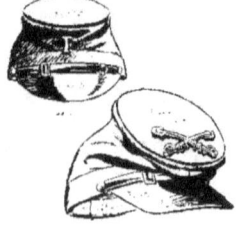

forage caps

Hardee hat

frock coat

sack coat

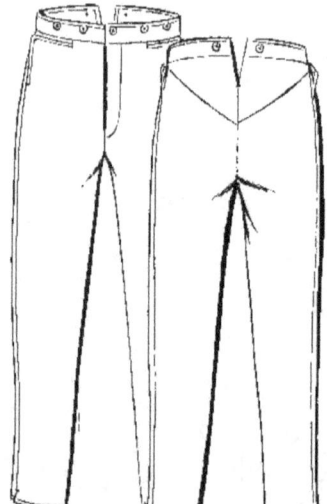

wool trousers

muslin shirt

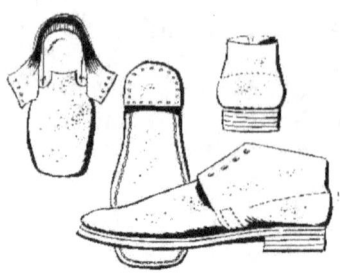

brogans

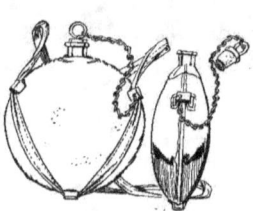

canteen

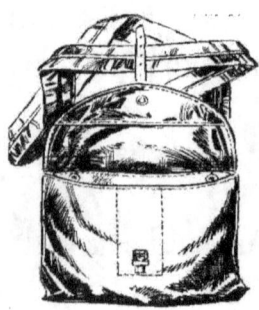

haversack

A SOLDIER'S KIT

A soldier coming into the U.S. Army was given the following items as part of his clothing ration. Think about what you might wear today when it's cold and rainy; then think about a soldier living in a tent or wooden barracks heated with a wood-burning stove. Do you think you would feel warm enough? What if it was hot and you still had to wear wool pants and a wool coat? Would you be comfortable?

Greybacks (longjohns)	woolen socks
Jefferson Brogan shoes	white pull-over shirt
sky blue trousers (cuffless)	dark blue dress coat (frock)
sack coat for general wear	poncho
head gear: hardee hat	forage cap with visor
waist belt with brass cartridge box on leather strap	cap box
	ammunition bag
canteen	haversack

Springfield muzzle-loader with bayonet

THE LAUNDRESS

THE LAUNDRESS

The U.S. Army in the 19ᵗʰ century was not like today's army. There were no enlisted women in it. It was an all-male army. It did offer an unusual position for a woman, though—camp laundress. She was the only woman who had any status in the army. Not even the officers' and soldiers' wives had it. Though she held no rank, she received pay and a daily ration allowance. It was less than what the enlisted men received, but since it was a requirement that the laundress be married, it increased the income of the family. Many laundresses were married to privates or noncommissioned officers.

The laundress did the laundry for the camp. She was responsible for the laundry of 20 men. It was very hard, physical work. Water had to be carried to the laundry area where it was heated in large kettles over a wood fire. Soap was shaved into the water and then the clothes were washed by hand with scrub boards and hand wringers. There were no clothes dryers to plug in. The wash was hung out to dry on lines. For this, a laundress earned $10.00 a month, 50 cents for each man's load. She also received housing, though it was often shared with other families. At one time, American Camp had seven laundresses.

Look at the picture. The laundress is standing outside with her husband and children. What household items does this family have? What tools does the father have?

Look at the children. You had to sit still for a full minute or more for a picture to develop. If you moved, it caused a blur on the picture. The children are not smiling so they won't ruin the picture. But do you think they are happy? Look at their clothes. Do they look like yours? What things do the children have with which to play?

THE ALL-PURPOSE CARRYALL: THE HAVERSACK

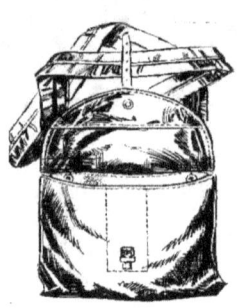

Materials:

large paper grocery bag
scissors
pens

Among the equipment issued to the common soldier was the haversack. It was 13 x 12 inches in size and was made of canvas with a flap and shoulder straps. Inside the haversack was an inner bag made of canvas. Generally white, it was sometimes painted on the outside. It was used by the soldiers to carry clothing, food, cooking and eating utensils and personal articles such as toothbrushes and soap. Candles, matches and writing materials could all be put into it.

How to make your own haversack: (Use the pictures on this page to help you)

- At the open end of the paper bag, draw a half circle about half way down from the top.

- Cut along the drawn line, then cut off the top flap. Next, trim any excess from the back flap so it is nicely rounded.

- Fold the back flap down over the bag. About two inches from each side of the bag, draw a wide strap. The straps should continue around on the back side of the bag.

- On the front of the sack, picture a belt and then draw a buckle and some holes to close the straps.

- Make a strap of twine or twisted paper so you can carry your haversack over your shoulder.

Fill your haversack with the things necessary to take on a camping trip.

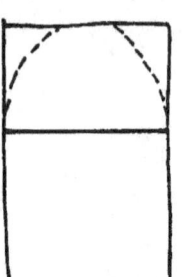
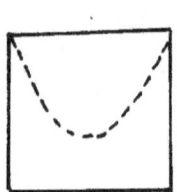
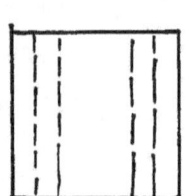
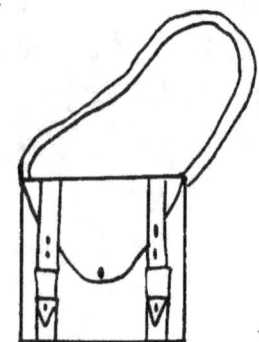

JOURNALS AS HISTORY

A journal is a daily record of events that helps people to think about important things in their lives and to remember them. Not everyone could read and write in the 1860s, especially a common soldier who might not have had good schooling or was an immigrant, as many of the American soldiers were. Fortunately, journals have survived that tell of different experiences in the early years of the British and American military camps. Read both sets of journal entries, then think about the ideas below.

A. A. W. JOY: A ROYAL MARINE'S JOURNAL

1. Joy provides an early descriptions of what would become English Camp. The trees and flat ground made a good spot to build a camp. Joy describes a large mound of clam shells. What does that tell you about the area? Had people been living there a long time? What do you think?

2. A few years before, a disease called smallpox had come to the islands. How would that affect people living there before the Royal Marines and Americans?

3. What else does Joy write about?

4. Locate English Camp on the map. Look at the early sketch of the grounds. In what ways are English and American camp alike? How are they different?

B. WILLIAM A. PECK, JR.: AN AMERICAN AT CAMP PICKETT

1. In Peck's first two entries about San Juan Island, what does he describe?

2. Journals reflect the language of the times. Discuss with your teacher what the phrases below might mean. Write the meanings below.

    a. "...our first officer is a **brick**"

    b. "...the men **pulled** directly under the guns...."

3. Journals often talk about the weather. Why would that be so important to Peck? Where was he living? What about his work on the fort?

4. Who else lived on San Juan Island? What did they do?

5. What other things about camp life does Peck write about?

6. Using the maps, locate the camp and Hudson's Bay Company's Bellevue Farm. (There was no English Camp in the summer and fall of 1859.) On another sheet of paper, draw your own version of this part of San Juan Island. Include Griffin Bay, Camp Pickett, Bellevue Farm and the location of the redoubt construction site in your picture.

A ROYAL MARINE'S JOURNAL

A.W. Joy arrived in Vancouver on the HMS *Tribune* with the Royal Light Marines in February 1859. Some of his contacts with San Juan Island are recorded below. Notice how he spells words.

1859	**28 July**	Embarked in HMS *Tribune* and went to San Juan Island, in consequence of the Americans having landed some troops there.
	19 Aug.	Returned to Esquimalt...

1860	**21 March**	Left the Barracks, Victoria, and embarked in HMS *Satellite* proceeded to San Juan Island, anchored for the night in Griffin Bay.
	22 March	Weighed, and proceed to the north end of the Island, and anchored in Rocks Bay.
	23 March	Landed in a bay completely landlocked, our Camping Ground being on a shell bank—the accumulation of "years", evidently, as it averaged ten feet high, from thirty-five to forty feet through by 120 yards long, it was the work of Indians, as they live very much on a shellfish called "Clams", and of course deposit the shells just outside their Huts, hence the bank I mentioned, the brush wood grew quite down to the water's edge, in the rear the forest was growing in undisturbed tranquillity, yellow Pine, White Pine, cedar, Alder & Willows in the low flat ground, are the general features of the North end of the Island.
	19 May	Went away to Mr Griffin's H.B.C. (Hudson's Bay Company) got into a Tide rip, and nearly swamped, obliged to put back and run the Boat into a little cove and remain'd there all day, at sunset went outside the tide rip, swell still very heavy, after rowing about 1 1/2 Miles put into a bay—beached the Boat and lay there all night;

1862 15 Jan   I returned to the Detachment on San Juan Island
where I remained until the 20 March, 1863.

1864 6 Sept.   At 6.30 A.M. Proceeded to and called at, San
Juan, boats taking in stores to the Camp. I
called on Officers and old comrades, bidding
them good bye. (Joy was now on a different
ship)

1865 3 Oct.   At 10.45 A.M. after dropping our anchor and
getting it up again, we made a final start for
San Juan Island, arrived there and anchored in
Roche's harbor at 5.45 P.M. fired a gun from
a boat from Marine Camp (English Camp) to come
off, which did in about a hour with Captain
Bazalgette. Governor and Captain went onshore
to Marine Camp, also the Master and Doctor
Bogg, with myself, in the cutter pulled with
marines. I found everything looking about the
same as when I left it in 1863, we stopped
there but a short time, as we had to be on
board again before captain....

AN AMERICAN SOLDIER AT CAMP PICKETT

Private William Peck, who spent time at American Camp with Lieutenant Robert's engineers, kept a diary of his experiences there. Originally from New York, he came out to the Pacific Northwest a few months before the Pig War began. He was sent to San Juan Island just as Captain Pickett was facing the Royal Navy in Griffin Bay. He helped to build the redoubt at Camp Pickett (American Camp) in the late summer of 1859. His journals give us a good look at the common soldier's life as well as tell us about a historic event. In the first two entries, the *Satellite*, a modern and very fast steam-powered British ship, had its guns facing Pickett's camp. The *Massachusetts* was an American supply boat. By September, things had calmed down as cooler heads sought to solve the problem of who owned San Juan Island.

Aboard Steamer *Northerner*, August 22nd

...Run into the Harbor of San Juan at about 7 P.M. While coming saw Chips engaged putting heads into hermetically sealed cans containing meats and now bolt heads, nuts and other small missiles, for the purpose of returning the *Satellite*'s fire should she open on us. M. French, our first officer, is a brick and swears he will hurt them a little bit with his signal guns, while they are sinking him with their heavy ones.

In Camp on San Juan Island, August 23rd

We transferred aboard the U.S. Store Ship *Massachusetts* last evening and remained until morning. The *Massachusetts*'s 32-pounder cannons are ashore, eight in all. We came ashore at 11 o'clock A.M, preceded by Company "I" 4th Infantry. While they were shoving off in their boats, the men pulled directly under the guns of H.B.M. Sloop of War *Satellite* and the musicians played "Yankee Doodle" for dear life. We find 4 companies of Artillery, of Infantry and ourselves, numbering officers and men, 500 all told. We are to maintain the honor of the nation and lick the British, no matter what odds (are) brought against us. There is a Hudson's Bay establishment on post here and the British officers draw many of their luxuries from it. The two national flags wave about 60 yards apart....John (Bull) has five ships and sloops of war and can put 2,000 sappers here in 48 hours.

San Juan Island, August 25th

We have engaged in laying out works for a fort all day....The Hudson's Bay Company have large flocks of sheep here, numbering in all 8 to 10 thousand, from which the British ships get their mutton. There is one tribe of Indians camped here pursuing salmon fishing.

San Juan Island, August 26th

The detachment has been laying out work on the fort all day... I thought during the night we were getting rain, the drops came on the tent so often from the trees overhanging it. This is to be known in the future as Camp Pickett, after Pickett of Company "D" 9th Infantry, who came here first with his company.

Camp Pickett, August 28th

(Our) first Sunday...in company with others, took a ramble over the island...stopped at settlers ranches and shepherds hamlets.

Camp Pickett, August 30th

...Nothing new or strange has taken place. I may mention, however, that by neglect of some one, our mess chest was left at Fort Vancouver and we are without cooking utensils, plates, knives, forks or spoons. Some of us have made wooden ones and use boards for plates, borrowing cooking utensil, as far as we have been able.

Camp Pickett, September 2nd

Weather continues fine as could be asked for. We are or have been during the day in charge of working parties on the fort.

LETTERS AS HISTORY

In the 1860s, if you were going to do well in life, you had to know how to read and write. And if you were going to keep in touch with friends and family, writing letters was the only way to do it—there were no phones, faxes or e-mail. There was the telegraph, but it was costly and suited for only short messages. So people wrote letters. It was a sign of being educated.

A. CARLTON ALLEN: A BOY'S LIFE

Carlton Allen was the son of Major H.A. Allen, the commander of American Camp from 1866 to 1868. He was nine when he wrote to his cousin Jimmy Riker on January 24, 1867. Because the mail only came once a week or sometimes not for weeks at a time, this letter did not arrive at his cousin's home in New York State until June of that year. Fortunately, the letter was saved along with several other family letters. Today, his letter gives us a look into history. Reading old preserved letters not only tells us something about the times they lived in, but something about the letter writer as well.

As you read his letter, what do you learn about Carleton? What does it tell us about life for a boy living on an isolated island in the Pacific Northwest? Read his letter, then answer the following questions.

1. How did Carleton entertain himself?

2. Carleton had several animals for pets. What were they? Could you have such a pet today? Why or why not?

3. Carleton mentions that he got a gift of paper from his grandfather. Why do you think this is important enough to talk about in a letter? Do you think paper was expensive? Why?

4. Compare your life to Carleton's. What does he do that you might like to do?

A BOY'S LIFE

Camp Steele
San Juan Island
Jan. 24, 1867

Dear Jimmy,

I forgot when I got a letter from you, but I am going to write to you now. Christmas Anson and Albert shot at a Target with a lot of other persons and the ones that shot the best were to have a Turkey. Albert got two. We had a Christmas tree. I got a sword and gun, trumpet, riding whip, a dog whistle, 125 glass marbles, a ball, and other things. We have skating now. I can skate a little, and we had some snow, and it was very cold. I got some paper that Grandpa sent me. We study every day until one o'clock, then we go hunting. Our Orderly shot a Deer, and the boys shot some ducks and Quails. Tomorrow is Saturday and we can go out in the morning and stay all day. They got seven Ducks last Saturday. My little Duck Jimmy went down to the hospital. I suppose he thought he was sick. I had to go after him and bring him home. Did you know his name was Jimmy? A great many crows come in the yard. One of them took him by the tail and pulled him around and last night an Owl was trying to catch him. I think his life is in danger. A boy caught an owl and gave him to me. (?) I have got him in a box and feed him, and last night he got out; but he does not go away. Deers are very plenty we could have bought one for a dollar but we had a half a one and did not want any more. This morning when I got up, I found my Duck dead; I do not know what ailed it. I am now going to have little pet lamb as soon as it can go away from its mother. Another boy and I are building a house for it, you must write me a long letter for this one. I write a little every day. How is Carol, and Clarence and Belle?

From your loving cousin,

Carleton B. Allen

B. MARY JULIA ALLEN: AN OFFICER'S WIFE WRITES

Mary Julia Allen was the second wife of Major H.A. Allen. She married him in New York and became step-mother to his three sons, Anson, Albert and Carleton, after their mother died. As an officer's wife, she had many responsibilities that she performed even in the wilderness of the San Juan Islands. Read the letter written to her sister in March 1868. In it she reveals something about life for an officer and his family. Look for things about life at Camp Steele (the name for American Camp after 1861). Does she write about the same things as Carleton?

1. Mrs. Allen writes about entertaining guests and providing food for them. What does this tell you about some of her duties as the post commander's wife?

2. Explain what these words mean:

orderly -

court-martial -

3. Using the maps in this kit, locate the two military camps on the island. Notice the roads and distances between them. If a horse goes ten miles an hour, how many hours does it take to travel between the camps?

4. Bridgett was a young woman who worked as a servant for the Allens at $35 a month. If Mrs. Allen had a servant to help her, what does this tell you about military life for an important officer's wife?

5. From what you might know about a soldier's life at American Camp, how was it different from an officer's family? Which life would you choose? Why?

AN OFFICER'S WIFE WRITES

San Juan Island
March 5th, 1868

My Dear Carrie,

I received your letter of December third a few days since. It took a long time to reach me as our mails have been very irregular this winter, the roads and river being impassable. I also got several from home. All came late and are telling us about their Christmas. How much you all must have enjoyed it and how happy I should have been to have shared it with you!

...It seems strange but this post is very expensive, more so than in San Francisco. These people do not stay with you. Only make a short call or a short visit, but here they come down on you for a week or more. The paymaster and his clerk have been here for ten days. We had to keep them ready all the time, although we could not accommodate them at night, and now here is a Court-martial and they are to be entertained for a week or ten days. And the boys went up to Steilacoom with a party for a visit and they brought back their two friends about their age for a week or two. And then there is always someone visiting at the post that has to be asked in to dinner, so though I save in bonnets and dresses, it goes in other things.

...On Saturday last we went with a party of ladies and gentlemen to call on the ladies at the English Camp, where we all lunched. Got home here about seven o'clock and I asked the party to come in to supper. Bridget had to have the chickens that were running around the yard caught and cooked and hot biscuits; so they did not come in until about eleven o'clock.

...We are having delightful weather now. I am sitting with a bright fire on the hearth and the outside doors all open.

...We did not receive our mail at the proper time this week; so it has just arrived ...I have been jumping and am distracted. The Major has invited four gentlemen from the Court-martial here to dinner, and we expected a whole sheep and fish, and of course are disappointed. Through someone's stupidity they have not come, so I did not know what to do, having only two chickens on hand and soup, so had to mount an orderly and send for some beef and canned oysters to make a pie...

...The party of boys have mounted themselves and rode down to the English Camp sixteen miles there and sixteen back over terrible roads.

And now I am going to close writing, not reading it over for I have not time...

From your loving sister, M.G. Allen

Notes

Unit Six

Settling
the Claim

SETTLING THE CLAIM

As the military camps went about their daily tasks, months turned to years and the boundary dispute was not settled. Representatives from both countries knew that ownership of the islands had to be decided because neither American citizens nor British subjects could rightfully claim homesteads. Until there was one civilian law of the land, those who broke the law would continue to take advantage of the confusion. On October 9, 1861, a **protocol** or agreement between the U.S. and Great Britain was made to refer the water boundary dispute to "some friendly power." However, because the United States was involved in the Civil War, the process was delayed. The war ended in the spring of 1865 and fresh attempts were made, but new issues had arisen between the two nations. The U.S. government was upset with the British government for appearing to have looked the other way while British shipyards built warships for the Confederate Navy. There also were issues about fishing rights that both countries claimed near the Maine coast. In addition, Great Britain was experiencing trouble with nations on the European continent. Still, on January 16, 1869, a **convention** (a more formal agreement between countries) was established to appoint a High Commission that would try to resolve some of these problems between the United States and Great Britain. However, the U.S. Senate did not approve it. Finally, in May 1871, a major agreement was signed, the **Treaty of Washington.**

The Treaty of Washington was an international first and remains an important example of arbitration. It not only settled fishing rights and Civil War damage claims, it also agreed that the San Juan Islands water boundary dispute would be arbitrated by an outside party, Emperor William I of Germany (or Kaiser Wilhelm I in the German language). Both countries could put their cases before him, and then he would make the final decision. To do this, the United States and Great Britain assembled maps, interviews and official documents. The maps and documents supported arguments as to where the boundary should go: Haro Strait or Rosario Strait. If Haro Strait was accepted, the United States would get the San Juan Islands.

On August 18, 1871, the emperor agreed to act as **arbitrator** or referee. After arguments were submitted by both nations in December of the same year, he submitted the papers to three experts in geography, international law and commerce. In September 1872, they gave their opinions. A month later, Emperor William announced his decision: the boundary-line between the territories of "her Britannic Majesty and the United States" would be drawn through the Haro Strait. The Haro was chosen because it was deeper, wider and more open to shipping. On November 23, the British ambassador notified the Secretary of State that the Royal Marines had left San Juan Island. The 12-year joint military occupation of the islands was over. More importantly, an argument over who owned the San Juan Islands had ended with only one casualty—a pig.

SETTLING ARGUMENTS: CONCLUSION

An argument can happen at any time. It may be a fight with a brother or sister. It may be a disagreement with a classmate at school. Or it could be two neighbors arguing over the location of a fence. In international disputes, arbitration is one of the best ways to achieve a peaceful resolution of a problem. Today on television and in the news, there are terrible stories about people and countries that cannot settle an argument peacefully. The result is fighting or total war. It is sad when people not only lose everything they own, but suffer serious injuries or even lose their lives. It should not happen. We all need to get along and when real problems arise, find a way to sit down and talk about them.

There are several lessons to be learned from the Pig War. The first is that disagreements should be dealt with quickly. It is not a good idea to let problems go unresolved. It can cause bad feelings.

Secondly, the old saying that "too many cooks spoil the pot" is true. The problem over the pig was not a serious one. It was between Griffin and Cutlar. When more people came into the picture, it became harder to solve. There were too many ideas about how it should be handled. Douglas, Pickett and Harney all thought they were right. Captain Hornby and General Scott knew there was a better way. It took courage to do the right thing when it was not a popular thing to do. For several days, Hornby was not popular in Victoria.

Finally, the best lesson about the Pig War is that there was no war. In the end, the dispute was resolved peacefully through arbitration. Although one country won control of the San Juan Islands, both countries were winners. The British and Americans together surveyed the international land boundary line and next resolved the water boundary by agreeing to arbitration in the Treaty of Washington. Today, the international border between the United States and Canada is the longest unfortified boundary in the world and certainly the most peaceful. This is the greatest lesson of the Pig War.

Question:

Think about a problem that you might be having with someone in your classroom, club or at home. Write down the problem. Then think about ways that you might solve it. Would talking to the person help or do you need someone to arbitrate like a teacher or parent? Do your best to solve it.

PIG WAR BIBLIOGRAPHY

General Books

McCabe, James O.. The San Juan Water Boundary Question. The Netherlands: University of Toronto Press, 1964.

Murray, Keith A. The Pig War. Tacoma, WA: Washington State Historical Society, 1968.

The Pig War: The Journal of William A. Peck, Jr., C. Brewster Coulter, ed. Medford, OR: Webb Research Group, 1993.

Richardson, David. The Pig War Islands. Eastsound, WA: Orcas Publishing Co., 1971.

Stanley, George F.G.. Mapping the West: Charles Wilson's Diary of the Survey of the 49th Parallel, 1858-1862. Seattle, WA: University of Washington Press, 1970.

Vouri, Michael P. The Pig War: Stand-off at Griffin Bay. Friday Harbor, WA: Griffin Bay Books, 1999.

_____. American Camp: A Historic Guided Walk. Friday Harbor, WA: Northwest Interpretive Association, 1997.

_____. English Camp: A Historic Guided Walk. Friday Harbor, WA: Northwest Interpretive Association, 2000.

Studies

Floyd, Dale. Comparative Analysis, American Camp Fortifications, San Juan Island National Historical Park. Washington, D.C., 1996.

Thompson, Erwin N. Historic Resource Study: San Juan Island National Historical Park, Washington. Denver, CO: Department of the Interior, 1972.

PIG WAR TIME LINE

1792-1839_____

1792   George Vancouver explores Puget Sound

1804   Lewis and Clark Expedition begins. Ends in 1806.

1811   Astor's Pacific Fur Company in Astoria on Oregon coast.

1814   Treaty of Ghent; end of the War of 1812.

1824   Hudson's Bay Company set up at Fort Vancouver on Columbia River.

1827   Fort Langley built on Fraser River in present day British Columbia.

1837   The Whitman's go to Fort Walla Walla to set up mission.

1840-1849_____

1843   Hudson's Bay Company set up at Fort Victoria on Vancouver Island, 14 miles
       from San Juan Island.
       First great wagon train leaves Missouri for the Oregon Country.

1845   Hudson's Bay Company places wooden plaque on San Juan Island claiming
       it for Great Britain.

1849   Crown Colony of Vancouver Island established.
       James Douglas becomes governor of Crown Colony, continues on Hudson's Bay
       Company board of directors.

1850-1858_____

1853   Washington Territory created; San Juan Islands part of Island County.
       December 13, Charles Griffin sets up Bellevue Farm on southern end of
       San Juan Island.

1854   U.S. Collector of Customs comes to seize sheep for nonpayment of taxes.
       U.S. Secretary of State William Marcy tells governor of territory not to
       provoke the British "on the disputed grounds."

1856   International Boundary Commission set up; surveying begins the following summer.

1858   Gold found in British Columbia; thousands of Americans come to area.

1859-1860

1859   Oregon becomes a state.
        Lyman Cutlar settles on prairie near Bellevue Farm in April.

6/15   Pig is shot by Cutlar; he goes to Griffin to pay for pig.

6/18   Hudson Bay men visit the farm.

7/4   20 Americans raise flag on Fourth of July.

7/8   General William Selby Harney goes to visit Governor Douglas on Vancouver Island.

7/9   Harney drops by San Juan Island; hears of Cutlar's problems; has settlers write letter to request protection from northern Indians.

7/18   Harney orders troops to land on San Juan Island.

7/27   Captain Pickett and 54 soldiers arrive at Griffin Bay.

7/29   HMS *Tribune* arrives in Griffin Bay under Captain Geoffrey Hornby.

7/31   Pickett moves camp from Griffin Bay to South Beach.

8/2   More British ships arrive with Royal Marines.
        Douglas writes Hornby that it might be necessary to land marines.

8/3   Hornby and other British captains meet with Pickett; Pickett does not agree to joint occupancy.

8/5   Hornby disobeys Douglas' orders; waits for his superior.

8/6   Admiral Baynes arrives at Esquimalt; cancels plans for landing troops.
        Harney directs Lieutenant Colonel Casey to move entire force at Fort Steilacoom to San Juan Island.

8/22   Casey orders camp moved from South Beach to present site; work begins on the redoubt.

9/2   President of the United States hears about the "Pig War" for first time.

9/14   General Winfield Scott ordered to go to Camp Pickett.

11/3   General reaches agreement with Governor Douglas to reduce forces.

11/5   All U.S. Army companies, except Captain Hunt's, leave island.

1860-1875

1860 3/20   Royal Marines land at Garrison Bay and set up English Camp. Cordial relations between military camps begin.

1861 10/9   Agreement between U.S. and Great Britain to have "some friendly power" look over water boundary dispute. American Civil War disrupts process.

1869 1/16   A convention appoints a High Commission to resolve problems, but U.S. Senate does not approve it. Angry at British over perceived Confederate support.

1871 5/8   Treaty of Washington. Settled issues left over from the Civil War and agreed that water boundary would be arbitrated by an outside party—Emperor Wilhelm I of Germany.

      8/18   German emperor agrees to be arbitrator. Appoints board.

1872 9/30   Arbitration board gives its findings.

      10/21   Wilhelm makes his decision. Gives islands to the United States.

      11/22   Royal Marines leave English Camp for good. U.S. Army command takes over both camps.

1875   Both camps abandoned. Property turned over to civilians.

LIST OF ITEMS FOR THE TRUNK

SETTING THE STAGE

Maps of northwest, islands
    and San Juan (overhead)
Sheep's wool
Picture of wool press
Bellevue Farm sketch
Griffin and Firth Diaries
Shepherd's hat

A PIG TAKES THE STAGE

Pig biography
Griffin & Cutlar biographies

FINDING A SOLUTION

Gen. Scott biography
Rules of the Game
"Project" of joint occupation

SETTLING THE CLAIM

Arbitration agreement
Picture of Kaiser Wilhelm

THE CAST INCREASES

Pickett & Douglas biographies
Extra! Extra! Headlines
Harney, Casey, Hornby, Baynes biographies
View of Griffin Bay
Pickett/Griffin letters
Hornby Writes His Wife

KEEPING THE PEACE

American Camp and English Camp layout
Pictures of camps
Diaries of Joy and Peck
Letters of Officer's wife and son
Canteen
Haversack   Rice
Cartridge box   Desiccated vegetables
Hardtack   Sewing kit
Toothbrush   Flags
Tobacco twist   Cartridge
Clay pipe   Minie ball
Bag of marbles   Caps
Playing cards
Forage caps
Tin cup, plate, utensils
Musket
Green coffee beans

Evaluation

Teacher's name:

School: **City/town:**   **State:**

Date of Trunk shipment: Grade :   Number of Students:

Reservation System:

1. How did you find out about this program? _____.

Please circle ensuing responses:	**(High)**		**(Low)**	
2. Was the reservation system convenient?	1	2	3	4

Program:

Relevance to your curriculum	1	2	3	4
Level of presentation	1	2	3	4
Appropriateness of activities	1	2	3	4
Methods of presentation	1	2	3	4
Appropriateness for class size	1	2	3	4

Please comment on the strengths and weaknesses of this program.

Curriculum Guide:

Overall

Usefulness	1	2	3	4
Quality	1	2	3	4
Interest level	1	2	3	4
Age appropriateness	1	2	3	4
Accuracy of information	1	2	3	4

Background Information:

Please circle your response: 1 (high/agree)   2 (medium/average)   3 (low/disagree)

Usefulness	1	2	3
Quality	1	2	3
Age appropriatenes	1	2	3
Interest level	1	2	3

Please list trunk activities used:

Trunk Activities:	(High)			(Low)
Usefulness	1	2	3	4
Quality	1	2	3	4
Age appropriateness	1	2	3	4
Interest Level	1	2	3	4

How much time were you able to spend preparing for this program?

Additional Comments:

Please complete and return at the time of your program or mail to:

San Juan Island NHP
ATTN: Interpretation
P.O. Box 429
Friday Harbor, WA 98250

(360) 378-2902
(360) 378-2240
FAX: (360) 378-2615